Mind
the Gap

Dedication

To my loving husband, my beautiful daughters –
thank you for your patience, support and
unconditional love. You are what drives me forward.

With thanks to my Dad who taught me my principles,
my Mum who helped me make them a reality and
my Sister who never questions them.

Sarah and Chris – I could never have hoped
for two more special friends.

Mind
the Gap
Creating your successful business strategy

SUSANNAH SCHOFIELD

KoganPage

LONDON PHILADELPHIA NEW DELHI

First published in Great Britain and the United States in 2013 by Kogan Page Limited

120 Pentonville Road	1518 Walnut Street, Suite 1100	4737/23 Ansari Road
London N1 9JN	Philadelphia PA 19102	Daryaganj
United Kingdom	USA	New Delhi 110002
www.koganpage.com		India

© Susannah Schofield 2013

The right of Susannah Schofield to be identified as the author of this work has been asserted by her in accordance with the Copyright, Designs and Patents Act 1988.

ISBN   978 0 7494 6878 1
E-ISBN   978 0 7494 6879 8

British Library Cataloguing-in-Publication Data

A CIP record for this book is available from the British Library.

Library of Congress Cataloging-in-Publication Data

Schofield, Susannah.
    Mind the gap : creating your successful business strategy / Susannah Schofield.
        pages cm
    ISBN 978-0-7494-6878-1 – ISBN 978-0-7494-6879-8   1. Strategic planning.
2. Business planning.   I. Title.
    HD30.28S3456 2013
    658.4'012–dc23
                                                                                    2012041102

Typeset by Graphicraft Limited, Hong Kong
Printed and bound in India by Replika Press Pvt Ltd

Contents

Endorsements vii
Acknowledgements ix

01 Setting the scene 1

The future state 4
The Dice Matrix Model: don't leave success to chance 7
Do things differ in today's business world? 10
Business and the savvy consumer: what customers really want 14

02 Lies, more lies and statistics! 16

03 Quotes from the famous, infamous and wise 57

04 Killer questions: their thoughts, your business 65

Whose business is it!? 67
The world we live in 103
The generation gap 138
Their secret views: your successful business 170

05 The world tomorrow: embrace the future 171

Marketing in today's world 171
Making money from technology 174
The mobile phone market: the future and your business 176

06   The world's gone crazy: a sign of the times!   180

07   The 100 Matrix: what people really think   184

The questions   185
The answers   186
The results   197

08   The Dice Matrix Model: time to succeed   199

How DMM works   200
Stage 1: tactical questions for customers and employees
    (first outputs)   202
Stage 2: strategic alignment of tactical results
    (second outputs)   208
Stage 3: gap analysis (third outputs)   212
One stage further: the 3D dimension   216

09   This way to success...   219

Index   220

Endorsements

Susannah Schofield has 20 years' commercial, sales and marketing, and strategy development experience in the corporate and SME world, and has acted both as leadership coach and ambassador for change. As a founding partner of a direct selling organization, she led the concept, brand development, strategy and delivery of the business. She currently sits on the board as an investor and consultant to deliver the strategic plan, and as New Business Commercial Director, leads a team of 200. Susannah has presented at many workshops and conferences on topics including motivation, team coaching, direct selling and new technology in marketing.

Endorsements from some of those who have worked with Susannah Schofield, and heard her present at seminars and conferences over the years:

As a member of our trade association, Best in Glass, under the leadership of Susannah Schofield, have proved they can really punch above their weight in competing alongside some of the very large multinational companies.

They are a young dynamic SME, learning as they go and prepared to be innovative and risk taking as they grow their business in a tough and challenging economic environment.

Susannah has proved herself to be a new breed of strategic thinker with her energetic and captivating leadership style.

Paul Southworth, Director General, Direct Selling Association

Susannah has so much to offer; she is intelligent, thoughtful, practical, determined, resourceful and energetic – the complete set. She has great natural gifts and high-level corporate experience, a combination which is very rare and highly valuable.

It has been a pleasure to know and work with her over the past few years – and at quite challenging times which has not deterred her!

Nick Mallett, Director, Nick Mallett Legal Consulting

Acknowledgements

With thanks to:

Geoffrey Dicks MBE

Asia Society Research on e-waste

Michael Zhao and his film and research on e-waste

All the surveyed 'anonymous' individuals

MP, PS, CK, SR, GH, JP, SC, JC and HS for answering all the questions with honesty, integrity and consideration

Various newspapers for the quotes and statistics

The Week for its brilliant roundup of news and quality journalism

Kogan Page for encouragement and total support

Morwenna and John for proofreading

Ben Hunt-Davis for speaking at the DSA event and for giving me a copy of *Will it make the boat go faster?*

Gartner Dataquest Statistics

Forrester Research in Mobile Communications

mobiThinking/Market Global

Graham Davis, for trusting, investing time and believing in me

Neil Cannell for being so very smart with numbers

My team for delivering and just being the best

Fiona Dempsey at Kogan Page for being so very helpful and patient!

Peter Reed, for breakfast!

All those who have advised me at Best in Glass LLP

Chapter One
Setting the scene

Sticks and stones may break my bones but regulation and legislation will kill me! Having worked for a large corporate company in one guise or another for a few decades, I started to forget how hard an entire business is to run. Large corporate companies have helplines and hot-desks: places people can go and sit, have meetings and drink coffee. There is time for conversations by the 'water cooler' about the TV last night and time for communication about aspects of politics, local papers and the latest celebrity gossip.

You build a culture within a large firm that enables every individual to work as hard as the next person. It allows people to be hidden by department and division. If I turn up to work and my laptop fails to start I call the IT helpdesk; when one of my team acts inappropriately and needs disciplining in line with business policy I turn to the HR department for guidance and assistance. When I need to buy something I go to procurement and get a purchase order number – these are often things I considered the bane of my life in big businesses. You can do nothing quickly as everything must follow 'process'. It can be like wading through treacle to get the smallest thing changed, or the easiest thing resolved. Extra paperwork, mountains of needless phrases like: 'I will give you a quick heads-up on the latest low-down to allow you to resolve your downturn versus quota, or target driven statistical data.'

You can end up having to read a one-page strategy paper three times to get to the actual hidden meaning behind jargon such as 'blue-sky thinking', or 'outside the box'. My favourite happens to be 'let's build a robust process around that solution'. Of course – who would build any process that was not robust? It is adding words to a statement to allow corporate justification, for people to gain synergy across a business. We all feel comfortable in our own business bubble of inane words and phrases, and it allows us to feel connected, to feel part of something. It plays to our egos and confirms that we are in the know. Osmosis is what gives our businesses their culture; you must be submersed in similarities to feel you fit, and find a business with the core values and branding that makes you want to belong.

After years in a corporate firm, being part of the furniture, I felt safe in the knowledge that I could, and can, talk 'business' as a language – but when I stepped away from the corporate world and turned to starting up an SME (small and medium-sized enterprise) I realized quickly that all SMEs have to look at life very differently. The language of a start-up business is not that of justification, it is one of survival – quick decisions made to gain tactical advantages across an ever-moving business case. At a small business headquarters you have the ability to change the direction of a business with a conversation that makes that business language so much more powerful and demanding. At a small business you need to be multilingual in business talk to gain any advantage – no one department has the hidden answers or advice; it is down to you to acquire that knowledge, and then to teach others.

My journey and my unique position allowed me to understand, to compare and to laugh about the differences and the incredible similarities and ironies of both big business and the SME world.

I hope I have created a book that will not only confirm your current business's status and understandings, irrespective of whether you work for a corporate or an SME, but will also allow you to understand how you compare in the market as a business and an individual. So, no matter what type of company you own or work for, this book will help you get the best from your division, business and sector.

Welcome to the Dice Matrix Model (DMM) – a simple business tool that will allow you to drive strategy through your business, informed by actual, physical outputs and performance from both your customers and your employees. It will focus your business and its direction going forwards. You can use the Dice Matrix Model on any size of business, at any time – in fact the more you use it the better understanding you gain.

The model was built after many consultations with small businesses and large corporate firms who needed, and wanted, to lead in the market – not follow. They wanted to be trailblazing organizations and the only way they could be such was to do something different. The Dice Matrix Model is an output from all of those programmes and projects – bringing to life a model that genuinely addresses the needs of a business irrespective of whether they want to grow, remain static or scale back to a more bespoke offering.

As a result of reading this book you will have a business model to use that will allow you to:

- stress-test your weaknesses as a business;
- test yourself against your customers' perceptions and the reality you provide as a business;
- carry out detailed gap analysis to identify your strengths against those of your competitors and their strengths, and thus move you towards more considered strategies;
- compare your business against your competitors and against industry standards;
- compare your employees' beliefs with those of your business brand and create a stronger foundation on which to continue to build your business;
- deliver more as a company by acquiring, retaining and growing your customer base;

- understand what customers want;
- understand the importance of data segmentation in a fragmented market;
- have the ability to take an objective look at your offerings as a company and address your weaknesses, push your strengths and succeed as a business.

Or maybe if I removed the business buzz words: once you use the business model you will be a stronger company, make better considered decisions, have happier customers and employees and make more money... That has to be worth a read!

You will be able to break down conceptions that things are 'too hard' or 'too difficult' as the outcomes will give you simple analogies that bring the hardest tasks to life, with easily achievable, bite-sized actions that make even the toughest goals seem reachable. Marketing, for example, is looked on as a fine art, but by remembering that marketing is just the ability to shout about your business, and that you must either offer something new to existing customers or something existing to new customers, it becomes simple.

It is worth noting that family businesses make up a quarter of the British economy; they employ nearly 10 million people but 1,000 small firms are going bust every single month. For family firms the risk is so much more than just profit, it is relationships and normally personal debt and risk. So don't leave your business success down to chance: start to roll the business Dice now!

The future state

by Geoffrey Dicks, MBE, Chief Economist, Novus Capital Markets

In 2007, after 15 years of steady expansion combined with low inflation, British businessmen and -women might have imagined that the next five years would bring more of the same, a stable

environment in which to develop and grow their business. If so, they could not have been more wrong. The Great Moderation, as it was known in the USA, or the NICE (Non-Inflationary, Consistently Expansionary) decade, as Bank of England Governor Mervyn King dubbed it, came crashing to an end in 2008–09. A crisis that started in the US sub-prime housing market exposed the fragilities of the hugely interwoven global banking system, brought banks in the USA and Europe to their knees, and gave rise to the biggest financial crisis since the 1930s. Five years on, the epicentre of the crisis has moved to the euro area and threatens its very existence. The future is a lot more uncertain than it appeared to be five (long) years ago.

Amidst all the uncertainty, there is one structural shift in the global economy that remains intact. The emergence of China as a global economic superpower is apparent. By the middle of this century, on present trends, it will have overtaken the USA to become the world's largest economy. This is more to do with its billion-plus population than its average living standards but it explains why India with its huge population is following hot on China's heels. And with many of Asia's smaller, but still relatively populous, economies benefiting from a huge expansion in trade across the region, the old American adage needs to be stood on its head: Go East Young Man.

The trend is already apparent in the UK trade data. It is more than 15 years since the USA overtook Germany as our single biggest export market. Five years ago, ahead of the financial crisis, UK exports outside the EU were only three-quarters as big as our exports to the EU. Since then non-EU exports have risen 60 per cent against 20 per cent for EU exports and the gap between the two has disappeared. No matter what happens to the euro area in the months and years ahead, it will remain a relatively slow growth area in the global economy. There will be far more export opportunities in Asia, America and Africa than in Europe.

I have always regarded the EU in general and the euro area in particular as a political, rather than an economic, construct.

The ambition of European leaders is to build a United States of Europe to challenge the United States of America and to this end the economic rules that were supposed to govern admittance to the single currency have been consistently flouted. Now that the chickens are coming home to roost, the answer seems to be to put in place an even more rigid rule-based system that will condemn many of the weaker economies to years of slow growth. Yet I still expect the euro area to survive and probably in its present format. In Europe politics trumps economics every time.

It is more than four years since the financial crisis tipped the UK into recession and we still have no recovery to speak of. GDP, the total output of the economy, is still more than 4 per cent below its pre-recession peak and, with the economy back in a double-dip recession, the shortfall is getting bigger not smaller. The picture may not be as bad as the GDP data are telling us since there is some buoyancy in the labour market and private sector job creation is more than offsetting public sector job losses. But early hopes of recovery have been disappointed and forecasts repeatedly downgraded.

Against a background of growth disappointments and a crisis in the euro area that the politicians seem powerless to deal with, it is hardly surprising that comparisons are being made with Japan's lost decade, the ten years of near-stagnation that followed the collapse of the Japanese property market in the 1990s. The similarities are clear – a drawn-out process of balance sheet repair in the public sector, where a huge structural budget deficit will require years of public expenditure restraint, and in the household sector, which has taken on more debt than any country in the world.

On top of all this the UK's population is rapidly aging. The baby-boomers that were born in the years following the Second World War will reach retirement age (if there is still such a thing) in the next few years. Providing this generation with health and social care in the years ahead will impose a significant burden on the (relatively) smaller labour force – though it will provide opportunities as well.

It is very easy to paint a pessimistic backdrop to the UK economy in the years ahead. The legacy of the financial crisis is still with us. Our near neighbours are seemingly bent on self-destruction. The outlook is for several years of sluggish growth. But within that there will be opportunities for UK businesses in the huge and rapidly expanding markets of Asia and at home where the challenge is to meet the demands of an aging population.

To all those who are gearing up to meet this challenge I wish every success. I am certain that this book will help them on their way.

With sincere thanks to Geoffrey Dicks

The Dice Matrix Model: don't leave success to chance

What does the success of the country depend on? According to the government it is growth, and to gain growth we need to support small business and encourage more start-ups. The reality in today's world is that it isn't that easy to set up a business any more: we create entrepreneurial mayhem with red tape and excessive rules and regulations.

If you wanted to start a business, as a driven, focused entrepreneur you would set out your vision, identify what needed to be delivered for you to achieve greatness with your new business idea, and start. Sadly, gone are the days of the biggest hurdle being having to think of a name, print business cards and stick an advert in the local paper. Now we have many more things to consider, but before you even start to address advertising and segmenting your market or audience, here are just a few things that literally stand in your way before you start trading:

- premises: licensed or approved by the council;
- phone line contracts, suppliers chosen and confirmed;
- a fire certificate obtained;
- electrical appliances checked and approved, and stamped with a sticker;
- a licence acquired to hold/sell/distribute many items;
- website name registered;
- brand identity and logo designed;
- IT set up: computers, printers, internet access;
- bank accounts organized;
- all bank transactions to be bank approved, verified, tested and safeguarded with firewalls for legal data transfer;
- company registered: Ltd, LLP, or partnership;
- accountant appointed to regulate Companies House requirements;
- VAT registration obtained;
- training in data protection delivered;
- trademarks or other intellectual property protected;
- insurance obtained to cover your product;
- insurance obtained to cover your liabilities;
- insurance obtained to cover EVERYTHING;
- HR advice sought;
- legal contracts drawn up.

What does not kill us makes us stronger – or eventually wears us down enough to become compliant and work through the system.

To start a business nowadays you need to be dedicated and tenacious just to bring it to its first day of trading, but once you get there, once you have your business ready to go, that is when the hard work really starts!

If you work for a large corporate business your pains will be just as acute: legislation that stops you from carrying out activities you feel you should; unions, industry bodies or ombudsmen who need to investigate and stipulate the way you carry out business; competition law to hinder your growth. As a large corporate the chance of international transactions is much higher so European laws must also be considered and upheld. The policies set within 'big business' can be just as hindering and time consuming:

- competition law;
- company legislation;
- health and safety policy;
- property management;
- IT set up: computers, printers, internet access, IT contracts;
- protecting your corporate image;
- protecting your brand identity and logo, trademarks and intellectual property;
- anti-fraud policy;
- procurement policy;
- FTSE share price monitoring;
- profit and loss accounts, annual reports;
- VAT registration and monitoring;
- data protection policy;
- organizing shareholder meetings and AGMs;
- insurance to cover your products, liabilities, EVERYTHING;
- pension management;
- maternity leave policy and cover;
- HR management;

- legal contracts/battles;
- financial management and control.

So one thing is for sure: once you have started your journey, whether in your own small business or in a large firm, and if you want to make what you do a success – keep reading!

Do things differ in today's business world?

Unlike businesses that currently face economic hardship, customers probably feel now they've never been so lucky. They have choice, they have the right to demand an excellent customer experience, but with that come cluttered messages, cash-rich but time-poor people who are so busy trying to keep up they sometimes miss the most vital things that are right in front of them.

Are we better off now than 50 odd years ago? In 1957 Harold Macmillan made a speech as he celebrated the post-war economy: 'Let us be frank about it... most of our people have never had it so good'. What he said back then was true; is it so true now?

If you work for a large corporation the chances are it has been established for some time, it has a legacy on which to fall back – a heritage that can help it keep its roots firmly grounded with tried and tested methods. Mistakes it has made and learnt from. However, the world is very different now and the landscape has changed beyond recognition – and not always for the good or for the benefit of business. If you set up your business in the good old days, about 50 years ago, then things were very different:

- The generation who went to university had no fees to pay; all students received a grant and most finished with a degree that was undoubtedly beneficial and with no debt.

- All dental treatment was free.

- Practically all companies in the UK were British owned.

- There were no congestion charges.

- There were no toll charges and few motorways.

- All the statutory authorities were owned by the public and administered by our elected representatives.

- You could only communicate via telegram, telephone or letter.

- The UK had a large stock of council housing to assist and home those that needed it.

- We were surrounded with seas well stocked with fish.

- There were no trials or lawsuits about human rights, where criminals now almost seem to have more rights than victims.

- People could do normal activities without fear of being sued.

- The nation's savings were with building societies which were run for their customers' benefit and not that of shareholders.

- Savings were safe.

- The UK had full tax relief on the interest people paid to mortgage companies.

- Married couples had tax advantages as opposed to the disadvantages applicable today.

- Our armed services were more extensive and, compared with the rest of the world at that time, were much stronger.

- We had many more post offices and a Royal Mail service that made a profit without a regulator.

- We had many government organizations that carried out research, built infrastructure and delivered other services to enable development in all sectors.

- We had substantial industries in farming, manufacturing, mining, ship building etc.

- The drug problem was much less serious.

- There were no speed cameras; instead the roads were monitored by real policemen who dealt with the genuine problems on the road of reckless and dangerous driving.

- There was enough prison accommodation to cater for those who deserved custody.

- If you contacted a business you would speak to someone in this country and your problems would be dealt with.

- A democratically elected parliament made laws and decisions that were not overturned by judges or Europe.

- We had large amounts of oil and gas in the North Sea.

- We didn't have the National Lottery.

- We could sell our house without the nonsense of the old HIPs or the new EPC (Energy Performance Certificate) costing money for spurious information that will only have to be duplicated later.

- Competent people could carry out electrical work in their own homes without having to pay to have it certified.

- Nobody paid for seeking planning permission or building regulations approval.

- We had a higher level of democracy, with local democracy in planning matters not being over-ridden, or with unelected quangos dictating so many aspects.

Now, however, in our brave new world we can communicate quickly and effectively and technology has never been so amazing. We have hundreds of TV channels free of charge, more if you're willing to pay. We have food choices that are beyond our wildest dreams; we holiday frequently, we have hobbies like golf or fishing or football that are a given not a treat; we have more new cars on the road than ever before. We go out for meals and get takeaways on a regular basis; we fly to other countries for business opportunities. We are one small world. But lest we forget the vital few things we have lost from the 'good old days':

- If you go to university you have fees to pay, no grants, only loans that have to be repaid. The debt can be considerable and many degrees are of little benefit in the job market.

- We have limited gold reserves as most have been sold.

- All our assets have been sold off: gas, water, electricity, rail and telephone services are now all owned privately, most by foreign companies.

- We are over-communicated to, constantly. Silence is rare.

- Our NHS and schools systems are heavily reliant upon Private Finance Initiatives (PFIs) where the annual costs will always increase.

- We have endless over-regulating quangos that make no contribution to the productivity of the nation, and merely create red tape and unnecessary regulations.

- We have endless examples of new projects or activities set up by bureaucratic government departments which make no contribution to the nation but spend the taxpayer's money to achieve very little output.

- We have leaders who urge us to save energy yet do little to really make a difference across the areas that would impact quickly.

- Tax relief is only given to those who have more than one home, and can afford really good accountants.

- We have a government/FSA/Bank of England/banks that lamentably failed to control the economy and have now committed our children and probably our grandchildren to unbelievable levels of debt.

Does it matter if our assets have been sold off? Well, take the case of electricity. When it was a nationalized industry our government could control it and formulate a sensible energy policy. But once in the hands of private companies any policy for the overall good of the country was not possible. The electricity companies used gas generation at an efficiency rate of 40 per cent, using up much of the North Sea reserves instead of preserving them for gas-fired boilers in homes and businesses where it could be utilized at 90 per cent efficiency. The only viable solution to our growing energy problem is nuclear power but any development in that field is now in the hands of private companies not our nation.

So, are we better off? They used to say in the 'good old days' you could leave your doors open without fear. Why? Because most people worked really hard but actually had very little worth stealing. We are not better or worse off now – we are just different. In business you have to move with the times, embrace the changes and the challenges that brings: if you don't you just end up looking at what went wrong and the things you've lost and not looking at what opportunities you have and how you could make it right.

Business and the savvy consumer: what customers really want

We are all consumers. When we talk to our bank manager and ask for money for our business, or ask any corporate investor to input a capital injection, inside they are all identifying with the product or proposition to ensure they would 'buy' the idea or concept. In business we must always remember that people buy people, but people invest in good ideas run by good people.

It matters not that you have the best idea ever, that your unique selling points are second to none; if you don't have attention to detail, good customer service and a cutting-edge proposition that moves with consumer demands you will not survive in this decade – no matter who you are!

If we look at those businesses doing well, and performing well above their competitors in this decade, we can list but a few phenomenal successes: Apple, Virgin, John Lewis, Harrods, Waitrose, American Express.

All of them score well above average on customer satisfaction average means score testing models; these are models that generate a rating on customers' perceptions of a business. Why do they rate highly? Because they all know the key to success is contented customers, consumers who will return time and time again. How do you always guarantee a contented customer? With a happy and approachable set of employees who will go above and beyond the call of duty. If you don't have them you need to stack it high and sell it cheap. I give you any supermarket chain.

So most businesses, irrespective of size or offering, need repeat business; they need to retain and grow existing business and they need recommendations, advocates and above-average customer responses. If you follow the Dice Matrix Model outlined in this book and address the outputs the model generates, you cannot fail to improve the business you own, or work in. We must listen to our employees and customers and address what they want. We should always push ourselves and our businesses to achieve more. As the rabbinical saying goes: 'Don't limit a child to your own learning, for he was born in another time'.

Or, in a different tone from Winston Churchill, quoted when talking about dinner: 'It would have been splendid... if the wine had been as cold as the soup, the beef as rare as the service, the brandy as old as the fish, and the maid as willing as the duchess'.

Chapter Two
Lies, more lies and statistics!

We live in a world that bombards us with information – we can see it all happening in front of us, we observe it but we must be careful when running a business that we don't just react to situations or information without understanding it. I recently made the mistake of listening to a few people within my business community and jumping to the wrong conclusion and thus an incorrect solution. Once I had announced the new programme of work we would undertake and the changes to be made I realized from the response of my team I had got it wrong. After careful investigation and a clear diagnosis of the information I appreciated I had jumped to the wrong conclusion too quickly and without being armed with all the relevant information. I will never make that mistake again. I am now confident enough to always take a step back and to ensure I take the time to consider all the facts and implications prior to pulling the trigger.

It is obvious really that time must always be given to considering the outcome of any decision or strategy undertaken. If we rush at a judgement call and do not look at the problem from every angle we can end up with the situation of more haste but less speed.

The information given to us on a daily basis is often dressed up as snapshots of facts that alone mean nothing – or could mean anything. Statistics are all things to all people. They can be taken in different contexts and with different parameters.

Remember – when you read or look into research, or when your employees or team members tell you something, or when your customers complain, make sure you really understand what they are saying before you react. After all, 77 per cent of all statistics are made up... or are they?!

The following statistics were sourced from individual newspapers or were found in the summary publication, *The Week*; all were published during the first six months of 2012.

> *80 per cent of managers think their staff are either satisfied or very satisfied with them as a manager – but only 58 per cent of workers say that is the case.*
>
> Employee Outlook Study/*The Daily Telegraph*

This plays onto why you should carry out the Dice Matrix Model application on your employees and your business. Gap analysis is one of the most important parts of any business – sadly the managers and leaders of some of the best companies around the world believe they are better than they are. I have always said people start to lose the plot, lose their way when it comes to leadership when they start to believe their own hype! Margaret Thatcher: love or hate her politics, she was a woman of many ethics and worked to a very high standard. Initially when she got into No. 10 she didn't have the place re-done from top to toe like so many of the new political leaders do. 'No', she said, 'not to worry, only Denis and I – we only need one bedroom'. She also bought all her own linen and crockery. When she was told she could claim a new ironing board – long before the 'expenses scandal' of the politician's world hit the country – she was outraged, stating it was her ironing board, and paying £13 of her own money. Why should anyone else pay? However, even an individual with such high regard for standards started to believe her own hype and by the end of her time in power she had not only started to look like her *Spitting Image* puppet but she had started to talk less sense! Believing in being totally invincible is very dangerous, especially in business, a fact confirmed by John Major, Tony Blair and Gordon Brown to name but a few of her successors.

Some leaders in business have a good run, they achieve objectives and goals and then they feel the need to stop learning, stop stretching themselves out of their comfort zones and just exist without the need to prove they make a demonstrable difference to the business. This is less frequently found in smaller companies as there is less 'hiding' room and more accountability; when a business is family-owned the business leaders can often struggle to 'pull rank' as they don't want to risk offending members of the family. However, it can be said most SMEs are aware of the need to deliver, both to their customers and their employees – as a result they retain staff longer and most are happier. Ignore the above statistic at your peril. If your managers believe their teams are happy, it's worth checking before you have a revolt on your hands that could cost you: are your managers simply believing the hype? After all, it can happen to even those at the very top!

Asked if they'd rather have supper with David Cameron or Boris Johnson, 48 per cent of female voters chose the London mayor, while 23 per cent opted for the prime minister. When male voters were asked whom they'd prefer their wives to dine with, 22 per cent said Johnson, 49 per cent Cameron.

Survation/*The Mail on Sunday*

This should confirm beyond doubt that men and women do think, and emotionally feel, the same. We just manipulate the situation to fit our own desired outcome – which sadly, is seldom the same! We respond to circumstances very differently depending on the set of criteria and the needs and wants of the favoured outcome.

Most of my friends are men. I enjoy the 'frankness' of a male conversation over the more emotive side that women tend to share when together – however, I have learnt that some men in business, as well as in their personal lives can be so much more 'sensitive' than women. I truly believe this is not a bad thing at all. My humble opinion is that gone are the days when you would want to employ someone who is proud of being aggressive. Ruthless, merciless, callous, hard-nosed, hostile, destructive and antagonistic are all words I have heard in my corporate life being used with pride. I have spent decades listening to boardroom banter and those who pride themselves on not working as a team, on being a 'lone wolf' that hunts for him/herself.

The world has changed from 'cash is king' to 'customer is king' and it has had to. Never before has it been harder to communicate with your customer base, from existing to new customers; the audience is fragmented, with many media options and channels to allow you to talk to your target audience. To survive in business today, to make a true success of any sized company you must be humble, honest, and full of integrity: not always the cheapest as Apple, British Airways and Marks & Spencer have demonstrated – but always the best. Putting the customer at the heart of everything you do. Being totally 'customer-centric' and not belligerent as an individual or a business. Those who claim that, when they are employing people, they 'don't want friends, they want business partners', are in my eyes ignorant. How can you build a business strategy around providing one 'brand and image' to your customer base if you don't like or respect the people you work with? When I employ people, I must always like them. I might not choose them as my closest personal friends due to a difference in hobbies, interest or outlooks on life – but I like them. If I don't, why should I expect my customers to?! People buy from people: face-to-face sales is still the most successful way of closing a deal quickly and effectively. Some businesses don't have the margin or the ability to use this channel to market, so other forms of communication have to work twice as hard for the same results.

I started my illustrious sales career in telesales. Training (if you can call it training) was a day in a room learning the 'AIDA' technique: ie 'to sell someone something you must first get the customer's Attention, then their Interest, then create their Desire for it, then get them to take Action'. So I went back to my sales pod and made call after call in a relentless quest to sell newspaper advertising space to anyone who would show an Interest, a Desire, or the vaguest Attention. Sadly after a few unsuccessful weeks, which felt like forever, I had sold nothing.

I looked at my basic sales training and realized it was not as easy as I had suspected. I started to listen to calls being made around me and then developed my own self-taught sales training, a detailed seven-stage process, which I built up myself to try to achieve greatness and better results. I ran the concept past one of the most successful sales professionals on the floor to sense-check I was on the right track and not missing something vital:

1 Understand the client's needs.

2 Demonstrate personal rapport and empathy.

3 Demonstrate reliability and consistency.

4 Develop innovation and flexibility in myself and the product.

5 Develop commercial agility.

6 Respond efficiently to crises.

7 Create perception as a trusted business advisor.

He listened to the system, nodded approvingly and said, 'you'll still not sell anything'. I was devastated. I battled on, determined to prove him wrong.

Defeat in those places was soul-destroying. Granted it is a very competitive, price-driven market that needed tenacious, driven people but if you failed to meet your targets – there was no hiding. At the end of every day those that had failed to meet their quota had to stand on their chair and justify to the room why this had occurred. (This would never be allowed now, not only due to health and safety but also one might suspect for fear of a bullying and harassment case!) It certainly concentrated the mind. After a few days of ritual humiliation he clearly knew I meant business and I was determined to stay and make it work. It was at that point he changed my sales career – with one word. He strode past my desk and said: 'Smile'.

I did – sarcastically – at him. Then I realized what he was really saying. If I smiled when I spoke you could hear it in my voice. It wasn't the humdrum sales patter of a desperate individual: it became a personal, friendly call which had meaning, real rapport, and commitment to the moment with that individual.

I have never looked back. It might be my hundredth sale of the day/week/quarter – but it may only be that customer's first experience of me and my business. It needs to be good, to be focused, and to be courteous – irrespective of whether it is a man or a woman – we all need a smile!

> *80 per cent of consumers have changed their shopping habits to save money, but only 10 per cent of pet owners have cut back on what they spend on their animals.*
>
> Mintel/*The Independent on Sunday*

Sales and success are only ever limited by what you believe and what you would spend. I believe at this moment in time I would never spend more than a certain amount on a handbag. I love handbags, but the thought of spending the value of a family holiday on one seems ludicrous – but people do. It is not wrong; it is just how they perceive value, and what is vital to them.

I recently went to a conference where the presenter got the audience to test its sales boundaries in an exercise to prove people will always buy, no matter the cost, if they appreciate the value. He wanted to demonstrate the only boundary to sales was our own limitation to value. Two individuals were randomly picked, questioned and then their answers were shared. It was amazing. Individual One would never pay more than £50 a head on a meal out; he was a stay-at-home, takeaway kind of guy who didn't feel the need for food. It appeared that Individual Two was a 'foodie'. He and his wife travelled the world to try the best Michelin-starred restaurants: £2,000 for a meal with high quality wine would not have been out of the question. If both had set up a restaurant, one would have said you could NEVER charge that for a plate of food; the other wouldn't have eaten somewhere so cheap.

Then it transpired that Individual One stayed home a lot due to his passion for music and his love for quality sound tracks. He had a home surround-sound stereo system worth in excess of £10,000. Individual Two had an iPod and a small £20 docking station. He liked music but felt that was money wasted: one sound was much the same as the other.

So, the real lesson to be learnt here is that just because you don't value it, or understand the power of it, doesn't mean you can't sell it. You just mustn't inhibit your own sales by believing the price is too high. Individual Two would have never tried to sell Individual One a £10,000 stereo, even if he had used open questioning techniques to find out he loved music – his own internal purchase value would have stopped him going for the close on anything over £500, as in his mind this was more than excessive.

We all have to learn, as depicted so clearly in the statistics above: some would starve first before their pets suffered. You may not personally – but that doesn't mean others won't!

> *63 per cent of voters oppose the decision to tax pensioners more; 22 per cent back the move. 36 per cent support cutting the top rate of tax from 50p to 45p; 56 per cent do not. 37 per cent think Sunday trading laws (which were suspended during the Olympics) should be scrapped permanently; 56 per cent disagree.*
>
> ICM/*The Sunday Telegraph*

A financial analogy. The taxman takes it all – eventually!!! Here is a hypothetical example.

As an entrepreneur I plan to make money – so I buy a property as I know there is 'nought as safe as houses' – or at least it is the best option in difficult economic times!

So I am now the proud owner of a spectacular new property, and as the new landlord I let the property with a new tenancy agreement; but as I have done it up with a fabulous new conceptual look, straight out of *Homes & Gardens*, I decide it would only be right to try to recoup some of my investment – after all I am an entrepreneur – when I let out the property. I put the rent up £50, so for the tenant to pay that he would need to earn an additional £100 as he pays tax at the 50 per cent tax rate.

So, the tenant earns £100, and pays tax at 50 per cent, so I get my £50. I then pay tax at 40 per cent, so the £50 reduces to £30 with an additional £20 going to the taxman. That £30 then increases my estate by £30, so when I die, 40 per cent of that £30 goes to inheritance tax, which is charged at £12 to the taxman, and I get to keep a whopping £18.

So, to date, out of £100, only £18 remains, which I leave to my children, who celebrate their huge inheritance with a cheap bottle of champagne at a bargain price of £18, of which just over £11 goes to the taxman in import duty, VAT and UK duty.

Ultimately, of the original £100 earned only £9 remains, and that is prior to any tax paid by the manufacturer on the original production of the bottle! So in a roundabout way the taxman gets everything – except of course our cheap bottle of plonk. Cheers!

> *Almost 1.7 million children aged 4 to 16 in England (21 per cent) are classified as having special educational needs. In 57 primary schools and 42 secondary schools, at least half the pupils are classed as having special needs.*
>
> *Times Educational Supplement*

This terrifies me, for two reasons. Firstly I am unsure how one in four future employees will have gone through the education system having special needs. Secondly, is this a justified statistic, as we have got better at tailoring education for those with different learning abilities; or has the extra financial supplement each school gets for every child with learning difficulties or special needs encouraged them to seek out and 'find' these children?

In the world of business every new company starts off with special needs – but after the first few years of trading or of a new product launch or project those needs change. Surely we cannot be in a situation where we categorize our young and they never move out of that assumed category until they leave education?

My father – who I am sure won't mind me sharing this information – went to an amazing school, but they got things wrong. At the age of 7 he was told he would amount to nothing – his parents were told he was 'backward'. However, he now, after getting a first class honours degree in engineering, happily lives with his wife of 40 years, he has two children and he manages to tie his shoelaces, eat without dribbling (mostly!) and has held down a full-time job since he graduated. Should he have been identified as 'backward'? No. Was this believed at the time? Yes. The moral? In business do what feels right, mixed in with what others tell you is correct. Never rely solely on the opinion of one individual: group consensus is great, but make sure they are varied groups. Those who look in from outside are not always seeing the full picture or the talents hidden beneath. If you believe in something then go for it: procrastination is the thief of all time, and nothing ruins strategy and planning more than quickly quoted inaccurate statistics, said with authority by those who don't really see the full potential of the opportunity.

> *37 per cent of the population are 'not at all interested' in football, while 19 per cent are 'not very interested'. The least interested age group is 18- to 24-year-olds, 64 per cent of whom say the sport holds little appeal.*
>
> YouGov/*The Times*

I love football, genuinely – maybe not for all the right reasons, but I still love it. The game itself is amusing to watch, what I call 'moving wallpaper': nothing too taxing but harmless none the less. But football buys me so much more than just the physical game. When it is on TV I get time to flick through glossy magazines, read books, write books and not feel guilty that I am not able to comment on the TV. Sport runs constantly in our house; if the TV is not showing sport or the news I would presume it was broken! Like every good business foyer or reception, in the kitchen we have a wall-hung TV quietly telling us everything we need to know on a constant loop. In the evenings when we have finished dinner my husband and I will watch some form of sport. Every now and then I will be required to make appreciative observations on the 'way he kicked the ball', the 'golf swing', the 'goal', the 'racing-track driving precision' – something will need to be admired, which barely breaks my level of concentration from my task at hand but, as it was designed for those people who wish to spend time together doing totally separate things, it replays the very thing I will need to comment on! I watch the replay, with interest and appropriate disbelief – make the right noises and my husband thinks he is the luckiest man alive – although... I may have just ruined that!

It also buys me the ability to never need to gen up on sport for any quiz, and most importantly and amazingly, I can pick my husband up and put him down in any one of my random professional circumstances: client meetings, conferences, charity balls, functions, speaker meetings – and with the international language of sport, he will be fine. He will fit in and talk about sport, it makes him happy, and the poor events bearable. He is, and I am lucky here, always open to take views from other sports fans. On a serious note football allows all strangers to communicate at any social event without having to discuss politics, money or the wife. Is the next generation going to tackle these taboo subjects – or do we live in a world of Facebook status updates so polite that conversation and debate will be a thing of the past?

Of all the things I fear our children and the next generation may lose out on it is ironically sport, the universal language of commitment, tenacity, drive, focus. To be a good sports person you must never waiver, never lose sight of the goal – never underestimate your competition and never look to be anything but first. Should the fact that football and sport do not interest

18- to 24-year-olds scare us as future employers? Yes – but not as much as it should scare those putting on networking events in the future!

> *11 per cent of people do not invite vegetarians to dinner because of their dietary requirements.*
>
> Warburtons/*The Daily Telegraph*

We, as human beings, perform our best when out of our comfort zones. We need to be pushed. The most successful people in business always look to work outside their comfort zones – that is when they are great. You seldom get uncomfortable whilst carrying out mundane tasks or things you know you can do easily. If you spend your career carrying out jobs and roles you know you can do – almost with your eyes shut – there is a real danger you never feel 'alive' whilst you do it, or get a sense of real satisfaction once it is complete.

We have all done it, avoided a task we fear may be either unpleasant or time consuming – it slips down the 'to do' list because it is not something we want 'to do'. Eventually it catches up with us. The task has to be completed – we have left it right to the last minute, we're up against the wire, just like leaving school homework to the last day of the summer holidays! However, once we've done it we realize it really was not that bad, and in fact the build-up to doing it was far worse than the actual task itself. The small voice of doubt we all carry in the back of our head made it seem so much more daunting than the reality. The worst element is often that actually when it is done and the 'huge' impossible task is now complete, most of us feel foolish about making such a big deal out of it, and then satisfaction is overcome by the inner thoughts of 'why didn't I do that weeks ago when I should have done it?'

I work with someone who loves to present, to get on stage in front of conference crowds of 500-plus people and engage them. Before he does this he rehearses many times, in the mirror, alone in a quiet room – over and over again, and about two hours before he gets on stage he is sick. He is one of the best presenters I have ever seen, cool, collected and full of inspirational, motivational delivery. I often ask him why he puts himself through the build-up, but he firmly believes that without that build-up, without being out of his comfort zone, he wouldn't have the passion to succeed, the fear of not delivering to the best of his ability, and THAT is what makes him great. Not the content, not the slides – the feeling of pushing himself to see what he can achieve.

We all get complacent in business – we all end up doing what we think we know best, but challenge yourself a little, try to push yourself out of your comfort zone, just think what you could achieve. None of us were scared when we were children, so why are we now? My four-year-old daughter is a sponge for information, my eighteen-month-old does nothing but copy her – would they be terrified of having a vegetarian over for dinner? The matter would not even cross their open, honest minds for consideration as a problem.

There are 300,000 mobility scooters on the UK's streets and pavements (up from 70,000 five years ago), more than in any other country in Europe.

Daily Mail

Wow – a sign we are getting lazier as a race, or is it that we live longer but our bodies don't quite keep up with modern science as much as they should? Are we getting larger and more obese so unable to move around freely without the use of mobility scooters? Do we as a country use disability as an excuse not to work and is this just a side line of that culture?

One thing is for sure, something has changed, and the only thing we can be equally as sure about is that in business you must never assume you know the reason for the change or assume you understand the outcome. Assumption is the mother of all mess-ups!

All marketing must be measured to ensure you get value for money: what is the point of paying 'search engines' vast sums of money every month to gain you website visitors if all of the visitors from that source don't actually buy anything? Why produce newsletters if no one reads them, why send out brochures if all your sales traffic comes via another channel? If it failed to work for you as a business a year ago things may be different now and worth testing again. We live in such a diverse multi-channelled market now that all companies need to look at every fact before making assumptions on sales cycles or uplift. Why does it take your business 30 days to close a sale, making your sales cycle from start to finish that length of time? Look at how you sell, what processes get in the way and how they can be addressed to make sure you optimize the sale and close every lead successfully. Can you cross-sell, selling other products to your customers from different ranges, or business arms? Can you up-sell and get people to trade up to a better product for more money if you spend more time with them – and if you do that do you make more money with a higher margin, or just increase the cost of sale so your margin goes down? How do you improve the life of your customer, do they always come back and buy from you again or is your business a one-trick-pony, and if so – why?

Ask the question, don't just read the statistic and assume you understand what drove that – coincidence in business helps, but we should never rely on it!

Around 131 million working days were lost to sickness in Britain last year, down from 178 million in 1993. The average worker takes just under five days off sick a year.

The Independent

This is great – those that are working, in the main, want to. People want to earn money and want to be part of a successful business. When you complete your Dice Matrix Model (see Chapter 8) and you realize you have people in your organization who don't want to be there – don't be afraid to let them go. We don't stay in personal relationships that get difficult and awkward so why should we in business relationships? Things change and not everyone can embrace change. Nothing is harder to work with than someone trying to work against you. Inside doubt in any organization can be the internal rot that brings the whole organization down. A 'mood hoover' that comes into any meeting and 'sucks' the enthusiasm right out of the room. People who believe things can't be achieved won't achieve them. If your results show you have individuals in your company who don't relish working for you or the business then cut them free. Long term you will be doing everyone a favour, short term it might cost you more to fire, hire and train but once you see what more can be achieved with someone who wants to work you won't ever look back.

56 per cent of servicemen say that, while wearing their uniforms in public, they have been approached by strangers who offer them thanks and support. 21 per cent say strangers have shouted abuse at them.

The Sunday Telegraph

As the great song said 'War – huh, what is it good for – absolutely nothing'. I would tend to agree, but I am very proud to be part of a country that respects and honours its servicemen and -women. It is easy to go to bed at night and believe that the only important thing is to provide money for your family, and to work hard to do that. Sadly a fair few of our fellow countrymen don't even do that, but these servicemen and -women provide not only an income but a way of life, guaranteed for the rest of us to enjoy. We should be proud as a country, proud as a nation and most of all respectful to those who allow us to continue our daily activities without the worry of what could happen.

The average six-year-old goes to bed at 9.33 pm, and the average eight-year-old at 9.49 pm. By 15, the average bedtime is 11.52 pm, according to a study of 2000 children.

The Daily Telegraph

I have always worked full time. During my first maternity leave I tried to stay involved with the corporate company I worked for; in my second maternity leave I set up a business that still runs today and provides work for other mothers who want flexible working solutions around their families. My children Brooke and Willow have both been in childcare since they were six months old. They have been at a small Montessori nursery that provides magnificent childcare from 8 am to 6 pm five days a week. It is a lifestyle that suits my children, as they are both outgoing and seriously enjoy the ability to learn constantly and to learn from others their own age. The nursery has taught them how to survive in classroom environments, how to make friends and how to get along with a mixed-race and mixed-culture group of people.

I am proud to say that, despite some criticism of the fact I have chosen to work full time and put my girls in full-time nursery, my girls have never been happier. It also means our weekends are sacred, special times that the entire family looks forward to and enjoys – no cross words, no one wanting to get out, or find excuses to do other things. In fact for 48 hours every week there is nowhere else in the world I would rather be than with my family, and I am not sure everyone could say that. Willow, my youngest, didn't get the first six months of her life at baby yoga, baby ballet and private swimming lessons like my eldest Brooke did. Willow was a child born into a family start-up business – she spent the first six months of her life in an office, being fed by receptionists – held whilst making phone calls and bounced in a bouncer on the main entrance door frame! Am I proud? Not really. Did she suffer? Not at all. Would I do it again? Yes but differently. Will Willow also feel she had the worst start in life? No – it was not a bad environment it was just that her experience was very different from that of her sister. Maybe she will be the corporate mind that goes on to shape the country in years to come and who will be driven by a subliminal inner voice that she gained insight into whilst taking her first look at the world from our office!

What I do know is that despite the guilt every parent, man or woman, feels, for some people working is a way of life. I also know I do what I do for my children, to provide a legacy to allow them to have all the things they could wish for – but I also do it for myself, I do it because I love the adrenalin of business, I love the feeling of success and the drive to find a way to make it work. My children are up every day at 6 am, because they have to be – therefore they are in bed by 7 pm, because they need to be. I would be quick to judge the statistic above and say that children up at that hour are too tired to ensure they do well at school, they don't have the mental capacity to make good decisions when they are functioning on such little sleep. I do need to acknowledge though that I set up a business with a two-year-old and a new-born baby; feeding every three hours probably made me a little less focused than I should have been but I don't really remember – I was too tired!

Should kids be up late? Who knows, statistics are thrown around all over the place that turn out to be totally incorrect. You need at least eight hours' sleep. Don't drink more than two units of alcohol a week, don't drink coffee, don't eat salt – all false, or true, depending who you believe or who you listen to. What I do know is that in a fast paced and quick moving world we need to adjust to the times, and maybe some of the best ideas occur late at night. For me the answer is simple. Kids should be loved, live in a great environment and be pushed to have values, morals and be polite. If they do all that what does it matter what time they get into bed – so long as they do so nicely when they are asked. I received a text the other day from my young niece, wishing me luck for an important pitch and at the end she said, 'Push yourself and remember – YOLO'. I had to ask what 'YOLO' meant: the reply came, and simply read, 'You Only Live Once'.

Around one in five Britons has a tattoo: 14 per cent of teachers are tattooed.

The Independent on Sunday

When we speak to our customers, we can never assume to understand what drives them or makes them tick. If you want to create a leading business you need to remain open-minded. Apple managed to trailblaze and literally rewrote technology and provided the world with a different way of doing things, forever. A unique way of storing photos, making phone calls, sharing the internet and e-mailing – but only because they kept an open mind. I believe that when the iPhone 4 was being created they needed to get the prototype slimmer and lighter, but after researching the technology and hardware inside the phone they realized there was no way that could be achieved. So not letting convention stand in the way of progression they looked at other solutions. The iPhone 4 is wrapped in a metal and glass casing – it was the metal that was redesigned to make the phone slimmer and lighter. They took the metal and actually broke down its physical attributes and changed them to allow the metal to become better suited to the end consumer. What makes innovation brilliant is often its simplicity, taking a task and making it easier, looking at something that bothered you and making it better for those that follow. We all learn new things every day.

We live in a world where things change on a daily basis. When I started my job in sales and marketing, there was no social media, no e-mail, no mobile phones for a short while – people worked differently and behaved differently. Now the world has embraced technology. We have agreed to allow people to communicate with us via many different methods, some of them, I think a little strange – you can imagine if text messaging had been created before the humble telephone, no one would be sending typed messages, not when the revolution of the phone actually allows you to hear their voice!

Along with a changing world is a change in stigmas. Thirty years ago no teachers would have had a tattoo; if they did they certainly would not have shared the fact. Personally I am unsure why anyone would take a design and commit to it forever, after all it is like buying a cardigan in 1980 and wearing it every day for the rest of your life – eventually you would wish you had the option to pick another cardigan. If your taste has changed at all over the first 18 years of your life, why when you reach 18 are you in a good position to choose something you will sport on your skin for eternity? I can be critical as, for your interest, I have two tattoos. Do I regret them? Yes. Would I ever show then at any function I attended in a professional capacity? Absolutely not. Does it affect who I am? Yes, it made me realize that ink on your skin is permanent. I appreciate the irony in that statement, but I don't just mean the physical ink of the tattoo – the time and emotional stage you were at when you got that tattoo done stays with you every time you look at it. The state of mind you were in and the emotional place you were at is captured for a lifetime on your body. Those that don't have them, now a reducing number in society, will be quick to judge others who do. A stigma is still attached to having a tattoo, but with 14 per cent of our teachers having them it is only a matter of time before the next generation will inevitably decide that it is 'normal' – just like having your ears pierced or your hair coloured.

I am always surprised when people out of context announce they have a tattoo – do I change my perception of them, even though I too have a tattoo? I think I do, if totally honest. Would I ever judge someone on the back of a tattoo? Not if I wanted to sell to them or engage them in my business. Let us not forget that many of the most influential and famous people with the largest amount of disposable income are covered in ink – their money is as good as anyone's. Stigma – translated means shame, disgrace, dishonour and humiliation. I bet that never crossed the minds of those at Apple, so why should it ours?

80 per cent of the English public feel patriotic when they see the Union Jack, but only 61 per cent feel the same when they see the St George's Cross.

British Future/*The Sunday Telegraph*

Symbols are so important – we love a brand in this country, a logo to make us feel special. People spend much more than the product is worth due to the brand perception and the logo. Never underestimate that feeling of delight and excitement when you leave the store with your chosen brand encased in all its glory in a logoed bag. After all, take a handbag. The cost of leather and the size of bag is all standard, design is limited due to functionality – but the price can range from single to high six figures. All down to brand.

Building a brand takes time, money, dedication, sometimes celebrity endorsements and always, always – luck! Even Aquascutum had to file for bankruptcy in 2012, and many successful brands teeter on the edge of failure due to the fickle buying public.

You want your brand to be liked, to be respected but never to become too big too quickly as that can result in fast expansion, the market may become saturated and you are left with over-supply and then under-demand. Crocs, the nautical shoe company, was, I believe, never intending to be such a huge retail and mainstream success – their near failure was making the shoes too resilient, so unless you outgrew them they lasted forever! French Connection was nearly a business out of business until it launched its FCUK logo and captured the minds of hundreds of people who wanted to be risqué – but once that became passé they had to think quickly, to keep up and change their brand and perception before the public turned on them and hung them out to dry!

As a business you need to understand what your values are: do you need a brand and what does it stand for? Many businesses spend a small fortune on shaping the company, making the logo look great, the telephone number needs to 'be clever', the e-mail addresses correct – but one wrong image in a paper, one badly answered phone call and the equity of your business is damaged, and then so is your brand. They say that if an individual has been pleased with a service or a company they will tell three other people in idle chit-chat – if they have been made unhappy, or had a bad experience they will on average tell 11 people about it personally, and that is before their Facebook status updates the world, or they 'tweet' your customers to tell them you let them down!

Logos are important to us as they make us feel like we belong; we need to feel part of the fabric of a business, a community or a team. If you spend time developing the brand strategy from the Dice Matrix Model you will only reap the rewards – build an organization with a clear brand and set of beliefs no matter what your size and you will only gain, keep and solicit other customers on the back of it. Guard your brand but never be precious or over-protective about it or you will lose engagement and connection with customers. Allow customers to be brand ambassadors – get your brand right and they will do this for you free of charge – and that is about as good as any marketing budget you could ever wish for!

42 per cent of the public say they are interested in politics – down from 58 per cent last year. 48 per cent think they will definitely vote in the next election, but 30 per cent say they are 'unlikely or absolutely certain not to vote'.

Hansard Society/BBC News

Engagement is really difficult – whether it be with your customers, your employees, shareholders or stakeholders, the art of any good business is keeping people engaged and informed about your business. That way they will stay faithful, supportive, involved and most of all affiliated to you and your brand. You want people to be advocates of your company – to recommend you to everyone they know and to be ambassadors of your stock. To live in a country where even the government struggles to keep people included and encouraged to become part of something that will hugely affect their state of finances, life and overall governance of the country, demonstrates how hard this level of inclusion can be. What could be more important than our political culture?

So where did the politicians go wrong – how did we end up with such a disengaged country all suffering from lethargy and totally preoccupied with other things? I believe this statistic is driven by the lack of delivery or accountability within each political party – people are not drawn to any particular party as the lines of distinction have been so significantly blurred they just can't decide who to side with. It has become harder and harder to identify with any one of our politicians – they no longer give views or answer questions, they all respond in a 'media trained' voice with the skill and precision of any well-trained lawyer.

We have lost the need to vote as we believe nothing will change – we have become so complacent about what will happen and who will make those choices we have lost the will to fight for what we believe in now. When Margaret Thatcher introduced the poll tax and people took to the streets, it was not just about the poll tax; that was just the 'straw that broke the camel's back' as people could no longer take what she was implementing or how she was leading the country. Fast forward to today: would people take to the streets? I fear not, I fear we would all quietly moan about how bad we felt it had got, but who would organize such a great outcry? The lethargy has become so pandemic we have forgotten the power of the people.

The problem is we don't really have democracy. The division into constituencies means that for some people voting will never make a difference. Take Sevenoaks, where the Tory majority is always around 20,000. If an individual spent a whole five years of a parliament going to and from their local polling station, able to vote each time, it would still not change the outcome. Yet somebody in another marginal constituency may change the outcome with a single vote! Voting is a good example of something we believe we should do, even have a duty to do, that for the majority of people is perceived as a complete waste of time – so we select the priorities in life we feel we can change.

If the country that you have set your business up in has failed to excite and deliver to its people, then take heed – keep your business alive, your proposition interesting, your range or service exciting and most of all keep your team or customers fully integrated. Let people suffer fatigue at your peril!

> *20 per cent of NHS hospital patients do not always trust their doctors. 15 per cent think the food is 'poor', 21 per cent think they are not treated with 'respect and dignity', 22 per cent suspect that doctors do not always wash their hands.*
>
> Care Quality Commission/*Daily Mail*

Trust is imperative – but it is built upon so much more than just image, brand or people – it is a culmination of everything. I went to a leading supermarket recently; all the tills were busy except the 'self-scan' option where there were two tills open with two people sitting chatting and not serving. I started to walk away but one of them called out and said, 'I can run that through for you here as no one else is waiting with the self-scan equipment'. Immediately that supermarket went up in my estimation; a single personal transaction had changed my opinion. Instead of seeing them as being foolish for having two self-scan tills that most people didn't want to use, a policy that would normally result in employees saying 'Sorry, I can't do that here – it's scan only', I now saw that this individual hadn't followed the rigid process ('the computer says no'). They had made it look and feel as if they were being flexible and helpful just for me.

Now, I don't normally shop in this supermarket but as a result of that one interaction I think I may return again. Not because of any amount of marketing spend, offers on TV or radio – my repeat purchase will be down to initial luck at just being passing trade and the fact that this store was quicker for me will, with the help of that one interaction, have resulted in a weekly shop for many years to come. Now the key here is to realize that fact, to somehow capture those moments and to thank the staff for working so hard and motivate them to do it again. Without that young lad being helpful, kind and efficient I would never have considered returning. Never under-estimate the value of people who represent your business. Always look out for those who do a good job and reward them for such a vital role, but also look out for those who are not helpful and kind as they may cost you dearly – and in more ways than simple trust.

Recently interviewing for a job role, we could not decide on the candidate – it was down to the last two but they were so close. We mulled over the decision and then the panel decided to 'sleep on it' and reconvene in the morning to make the judgement call. On the way out I was thinking which candidate I felt was more approachable, more people-focused to lead the large team. As I walked past reception I took a moment to speak to the two lovely ladies who smile every morning at me when I sign in as we exchange pleasantries. I asked which candidate they would employ. 'Me? – why are you asking me?' one replied. The reason was that I believed that the candidates would have put on certain airs and graces at various parts of the day and through-out the assessment – but when they entered the building and signed in they would have not yet stepped into 'interview mode' and would have revealed their true persona. True enough both ladies chose the same candidate saying they were friendly and polite whilst the other candidate was rude, crass and looked down their nose at them. I made my judgement on that fact. You can perform well if under pressure – but it is those un-managed moments of time that make people and businesses successful. Those moments of brilliance that drive customers and employees to stay loyal and to trust a business to grow with them and their needs.

More households in India have a mobile phone than have a toilet. Ten years ago, fewer than 4 per cent of rural households had a mobile phone: now 54 per cent do.

The Times

I have always said I would never go on holiday again without running water – for me I need to know I can wash and flush without any difficulties or it's just not a holiday! However, when given the choice of technology or running water, I am clearly in the minority! I understand the rural growth in mobile phones: as services get better and ranges become more prolific people can get better service so as a result the growth is organic. What I struggle to understand is the need for a phone more than a toilet!

On a very serious note, this statistic raises a huge issue. If you think of industrial or commercial pollution your mind automatically focuses on the coal, steel or oil industries; we picture smoggy skies, dirty water and toxic waste being poured into our rivers and streams. However, as we move with the times we must all acknowledge these visions may well become a thing of the past – or certainly a vision of less concern given what is now the king of pollution. Our digital world produces a huge amount of what is referred to as 'e-waste' – mobile phones, laptops, MP3 players, PCs – they all conjure up images of manufacturing facilities and technical labs where only the bright and genius work. Sadly Silicon Valley is now only a picturesque dream in what in reality is a terrible, toxic nightmare.

Electronic waste, e-waste, e-scrap or Waste Electrical and Electronic Equipment (WEEE) are terms describing discarded electrical or electronic devices. There is a lack of consensus as to whether the terms should apply to resale, reuse, and refurbishing industries, or only to product that cannot be used for its intended purpose.

Phones and computers contain dangerous metals like lead, cadmium and mercury – which can and do contaminate the air and water of those who have to live with the carcasses of our commercial waste. Now this may not seem like a concern to you or me, or to your business, but *au contraire* – the importance of following the directives that drive the safe recycling or disposal of these products will be very important moving forwards. Important not only for your own self-worth as an individual but also for the reputation of your business as this issue will only grow as our need for gadgets and improvement thrives. The United States is the worst culprit for producing e-waste, but it all ends up elsewhere, mostly in developing nations such as China, India and Nigeria. Rich countries have been shipping garbage for years. In these countries the poor, often including children, are stripping the components out of phones and dumped PCs and taking the valuable metals from inside – which are also toxic. The children are often breathing in the fumes as the metals are melted down in closed rooms, with no ventilation and little protection. What can't be recycled to make any money is dumped, turning rivers into poisonous, black, oil-like toxic areas.

There is a lot of it – the world produces 20 to 50 million tonnes a year, according to the UN – enough to load a train that would stretch around the world.

A journalist connected with the Asia Society, Michael Zhao, travelled to Guiyu in China, a city that processes up to 1 million tonnes of electronic garbage a year, to film a documentary on the impact of e-waste. 'I saw people putting leftover parts on coal-fired stoves, to melt down the waste to get to the gold', he says. 'It'd produce a reddish smoke that was so strong I couldn't stand there for more than a couple of minutes before my eyes would just burn.' Urban China is so polluted that few Chinese escape without some damage to their health, but Zhao says that local researchers have found that the children of Guiyu fare worse than their counterparts in nearby cities, suffering from respiratory illnesses traced back to e-waste.

The Basel Convention on the Control of Transboundary Movements of Hazardous Wastes and their Disposal was established by the UN in 1989 to control the hazardous garbage flowing from rich countries to poor ones. The convention allows countries to unilaterally ban the import of waste, and requires exporters to get the consent of destination countries before they send trash abroad. But the United States, a prime source of electronic and other toxic waste, never signed up to the treaty, leaving it weakened, and some of the destination nations – most prominently China – quietly allow the dumping to continue, for the money it brings in.

One solution is to promote recycling programmes for old PCs and phones, as Dell has done recently, or try to reduce the amount of toxic metals used in those products, as Apple has done. The answer will almost certainly have to come from rich importers – for poor nations, the money that can be made off the e-waste trade is simply too good to abandon, despite the environmental and health costs.

Electronic waste now makes up five per cent of all municipal solid waste worldwide, nearly the same amount as all plastic packaging, but much more hazardous. Not only developed countries generate e-waste; Asia discards an estimated 12 million tonnes each year.

E-waste is now the fastest growing component of the municipal solid waste stream because people are upgrading their mobile phones, computers, televisions, audio equipment and printers more frequently than ever before. Mobile phones and computers are causing the biggest problem because they are replaced most often.

> *79 per cent of British pensioners now own their homes, up from 62 per cent in 1991; 14 per cent of 16- to 24-year-olds do, down from 36 per cent. The number of unemployed 16- to 24-year-olds has risen by 50 per cent in the past decade, to 1 million.*
>
> *The Sunday Times*

A sign we live longer and better at one end of our lives than the other, that although we are an aging population, it is the youngsters who have to struggle more? The late 80s were heralded as the hardest time to be young and get a job, but is that no longer the truth?

Maybe it is due to the fact more people go to university so they earn less at the beginning of their lives, but end up earning more so they can afford to buy their homes? Who knows what really falls out of this statistic, except that the Brits own more homes than most countries, especially in Europe whose citizens mainly opt to rent as opposed to buy. We like to put our hard earned cash into bricks and mortar – to feel we are investing in something for our future, for our children's future; if we didn't do this as a matter of course the government wouldn't bother upholding inheritance tax, as the bulk of this always comes from property.

The number of unemployed should worry us as a nation and as employers. Do we want to see young people unable to gain access into the job world? No, after all, these should be the people who will be paying into pensions in years to come, the people we will be relying upon in our retirement to keep the wheels of commerce turning.

I believe the only way to address this is to bring back the good old apprenticeship – not the current Apprentice Scheme introduced recently by the government, with so much red tape and detail it makes any sensible employer terrified to take someone on for fear of being obliged to keep them on forever, irrespective of attitude or aptitude – or the fear of legal action if they are not given the training they believe they require or are due. We need to ask people if they want to work, get them into a role where they can get practical experience and a wage to allow them to live and get by – always with the option to stay on once they are able to complete the job with a level of competency. This is the only way we will get our young into businesses and enthusiastic about working. Too many people believe they don't stand a chance of getting a job – and with that belief you can only ever fail.

15 per cent of regular drug users admit to having taken 'mystery white powder' without knowing what the substance was. A third of those took it from a stranger. 53 per cent have taken cannabis in the last month, 34 per cent MDMA [ecstasy], 22 per cent cocaine and 20 per cent 'legal highs'.

Global Drug Survey/*The Guardian*

Well, when it comes to having fun, apparently we have no need for reassurance – we are totally risk-averse. In business this doesn't work; customers need to feel confident and trust your business if they are ever to place an order with you. Research shows that people will pay a premium of up to 10 per cent just to buy from a recognized supplier, even for the smaller purchase amounts. Office supply sales are often driven by trust and the usual website that your customer is familiar with; they don't want to go to the effort of using another site. It is worth categorizing your business for this very reason: are you a luxury purchase website where people enjoy browsing and seeing the images? Are you a functional purchase or a necessity supply rather than a rewarding spend? Either way you need to play your market accordingly. If you are a supplier of necessity, ink cartridges, office supplies etc, then you need to market yourself as time-conscious, easy-ordering, with recognition of the last purchase to save customers checking it's the correct cartridge again – all these little elements tie customers into your site and make their experience with you so much easier or better than with your competitors. However, if you are a luxury sale where individuals enjoy to browse, to look at the options and consider the purchase, you need to be aware that they will potentially look to other sites. There is no rush so they have the time to be able to look into what added extras you or your competitors offer. So when that purchase finally takes place – how will you make your site 'sticky' so that people want to come back and revisit the site next time they are in the market for such goods?

For example, in the simplest terms, when someone orders something online they want to know the order has gone through correctly, they require an e-mail saying the items are about to be dispatched and that they should receive them promptly and without any disruption to plans. The better informed you keep your customers the better your customers will stay involved with your business, even if the news is bad. People want to understand how and why things have gone wrong – they want to be kept in the loop and informed without the need for chasing updates. Customers want the service they have paid for – if it is cheap and cheerful then they won't be expecting it to arrive with a ribbon tied around the box, but if the item was sold gift-wrapped, make sure it is, and that the wrapping is above and beyond what you suggested it would be. By over-delivering you will get repeat orders time and time again.

The same philosophy works with staff and team members – if you want your teams to stay engrossed with the job they do well and totally absorbed into your business you just need to keep them informed and aware of what is happening. People feel in control if they are well-versed and knowledgeable about the future plans and wellbeing of their environment. So unless you are selling illegal substances then I suggest most customers are not as easily influenced or as quick to make rash decisions as your average regular drug user appears to be!

40 per cent of NHS staff say they would not recommend treatment at the hospitals and clinics where they work to their friends or family.

Department of Health/*The Guardian*

This is the real crux of the Dice Matrix Model. If your employees would not recommend your services or products to their friends and family then you have real issues. No one wants to work in an atmosphere or setting that is not conducive to their own values. Businesses never really let the rot become so endemic in an office – but we all need to be constantly aware that people's concept of your business is what they will portray when they sell it, talk about it or recommend it.

The fact that 40 per cent of NHS staff wouldn't recommend where they work is a really sad reflection of how little we now try to change the system. Instead of making the surroundings better, these employees all feel 'done to'; they feel unable to change anything due to regulation and targets. Big Brother is an important factor in business; you need to know you are getting value for money from your employees but you also need to allow them to be entrepreneurial to get the best from them. If you let people be creative and find new ways to work you will reap the rewards. After all, when most consultants come into any business, they usually have the foresight to rely on those who work there to give them the insight into any solutions they propose. They provide an objective look at issues, but if you can't afford a consultant, at least try to empower your people to find better solutions to the job they do every day. They may just need guidance and advice to ensure that any changes they make take into consideration any overarching and long-term effects, which in turn do not bring another area of the business to its knees.

In a perfect world you would want anyone who works for you to be your biggest advocate – to be your business ambassador – but the least you would require is a little recommendation. After all, no business happens without people – so if you don't want to recommend what you do and the service you offer, you are not doing your job properly.

12 per cent of GPs think the NHS reforms will make things
'noticeably better' – down from 23 per cent last September.

ComRes/BBC

The biggest lesson I ever learnt in business was exactly this: you must always keep your business stakeholders or shareholders on side – not just informed and cognizant of future plans, strategies or activities but 100 per cent delighted and ecstatic with future plans. Your customers should be at the heart of everything you do as without them you don't have a business, BUT your stake- and shareholders are the reason you make money and without them your business would also potentially fail.

Many years ago we secured some sponsorship for a local event; it wasn't a huge deal but it helped us put the event on without eating into the income raised, plus the local company was very excited about the prospect of targeting all the attendees. We worked hard as a team of inexperienced events co-ordinators.

We looked at what the target audience for the event was, the age range attending, what they liked to buy, how they liked to be marketed to and pulled together a very comprehensive offering to any potential sponsor. As a result we very quickly secured our sponsor and signed all the paperwork. The money was banked and we got on with the real job, organizing the event. We failed miserably to keep our sponsor content and happy: we were so busy setting up the event we failed to realize the key to getting sponsorship and making it really work is not to win the money and then believe the relationship is sealed, but to keep the romance alive. The signed deal is not the end of the courtship – it is just the beginning, it is the time when you really need to invest in that person/company and ensure they believe in your goals, vision and concept. That way they in turn will put more back into the partnership to ensure it blossoms.

The same goes for shareholders – you can't just take the investment and walk away. But even more important are stakeholders, people or companies who might not actually have any 'skin in the game' or exposure to financial outlay but without whose support the entire project may be at risk. The NHS reforms look like they are struggling to gain support, the government failed to engross their stakeholders enough, and as a result they look like they have failed to gain not only active participation but also credibility as a project due to the diminishing involvement and participation of those who will be used to deploy the programme – the stakeholders.

So be warned – you need your customers, but customers will only come if your business has a great reputation and credibility, and you need to remember who you need to keep jubilant to enable you to deliver.

42 per cent of Britons would 'seriously consider' emigrating: 6 per cent are 'actively planning' it. 52 per cent see the cost of living as a reason to move abroad, while 37 per cent say the weather is the reason. 11 per cent think 'British people' are a good reason to leave Britain.

YouGov/*The Sunday Times*

'Will the last person to leave please turn out the lights?' That of course was said in the election day headline in 1992 in *The Sun* about the Labour government and Neil Kinnock in particular. It has been reused and rehashed many times since then, but back in 1992 it was considered inevitable that we would have power to turn off... In 2012 we are not so sure; energy is in crisis and costing a fortune, and the world has changed since then. In 1992 the famous post-election front-page headline of Saturday 11 April claimed 'It's The Sun Wot Won It'. In those simpler times a newspaper claimed the attention of most people. Only four channels to watch on TV, limited mobile communications and a much more vocal UK, able to articulate the way it felt about issues and economies. To have 42 per cent of Britons thinking about potentially moving on must send a shot across the bows for any country. If any business had an attrition rate as high as 6 per cent even actively looking for another job at any time it would be cause for concern, especially if 11 per cent were moving on simply to get away from their own team members!

We need to speak up – we need to start to get a sense of community back into this country and that needs to be led by businesses, both large and small. Some fantastic work is starting to happen across the country. Starbucks have a 'community team' which volunteer in Starbucks' uniforms to clean the streets of London. They recently also ran a marketing campaign giving everyone a free coffee if they came into a store on a certain day and introduced themselves – a brilliant way of building a community around a business. The 'broken society' we all freely refer to will not be fixed by governments and initiatives from local councils – it must be down to business and local community businesses to drive that fundamental change and put in infrastructures to allow people to feel part of something. Over time we will hopefully get back to a sense of belonging where many more people want to stay than leave!

> *55 per cent of the world's pigs live in China. The Chinese smoke*
> *38 per cent of the cigarettes consumed in the world.*
>
> The Guardian

These two facts strike me as strange statistics; they surprise me, but the second fact confirms beyond doubt the value of marketing, and with one small statistic guarantees it works! Let me explain...

Throughout time and the history of the advertising world there has hardly been a topic more controversial than tobacco advertising or sponsorship. China, which is both the world's largest producer and consumer of tobacco has been tightening tobacco regulation over the past seven years, but in this country you can clearly see the effect of tobacco advertising on its people.

Since a protective Convention on Tobacco Control was established in 2005, anti-smoking campaigners have been looking to reduce tobacco consumption through laws banning cigarette advertising and sponsorships, making cigarettes less accessible to the youth and prohibiting smoking in public places.

In China, where marketing has been rife, consumers inhale an estimated one in every three cigarettes smoked globally – this in a country where one in three cigarettes are both produced and consumed.

Direct advertising is not the only concern; smoking scenes on Chinese television channels are very frequent, and tobacco control supporters worry that Chinese youth could be led to smoke through this indirect tobacco promotion, without a clear understanding of the health risks involved.

We should not forget that China is a very traditional and cultural society where age-old cultural traditions, like that of giving cigarettes as gifts, will also potentially perpetuate the promotion of tobacco.

While advertising executives may argue that China's economy is largely dependent on the tobacco industry, the medical expenditure and productivity loss of smokers suffering the ill-effects of cigarettes are also on the rise. Tobacco control officials have called for a ban on tobacco advertising, a decrease in on-screen smoking scenes and the establishment of public education campaigns to make Chinese consumers fully aware of the dangers of smoking.

The question is: will this work?

Do we need to cover up tobacco in newsagents in the UK – is it the visual boxes and colours that attract youngsters to smoke? I think not: it is culture, peer pressure – the belief that it is 'cool' from years of films and 'tough guys' looking like they are in control and powerful. To have gravitas you must smoke. Now the times are changing, you have to go outside, in the rain – it is no longer sophisticated to be huddled under an awning taking a drag from your ciggie. This will be the reason youngsters stop smoking.

As an aside – when you think of Chinese food, you never think of pork, ham or bacon! And China is also the world's largest wine producer, yet we would never consider them as creating good wine. The reason – they make it, keep it and consume it. Sensible!

Complaints against nurses – recorded by the Nursing and Midwifery Council – rose 139 per cent between 2008/9 and 2010/11.

The Independent

Is this due to a more litigious society – are we more willing to complain about services; or is this in fact a reflection of businesses across the UK? Do individuals expect a better level of service now? Do businesses step up to provide that excellent service which means that other, more practical and functional (I term this 'perfunctional') services are no longer held in such esteem?

It could be reflected in the ease of communication tools. Gone are the days when you have to find an address, type and print a letter, find an envelope and a stamp and a post box – now at the flick of a button you can find a website, an e-mail address and send a complaint in a couple of minutes. Are we as a nation more aggrieved, or it is just easier to tell people we are? Do we cover our backs and register our disapproval – just in case? Do we look for better quality because our industries and business sectors have raised the game so much and standards are so high? Maybe it's a mixture of all of those things, but one thing is for sure – if your business isn't receiving any feedback then your customers are not bought into your brand. It is better to know what to put right than to have no one bother to tell you it is wrong.

> *Every year 18,000 children in Bangladesh die from drowning – more than from tuberculosis, tetanus, whooping cough, malaria and polio put together.*
>
> *The Independent*

I am always amazed and deeply saddened that the world is so very different across each continent. The famine and extreme circumstances people have to live with are so very different depending on where on this earth you derive. Some businesses give great support to charities; tax efficient the cynical say, but charities themselves do much hard work to support the issues others face. This is a stark reminder to me that when I lie awake at night and worry about finances and the other issues I face (although in my universe they are imperative), I actually need to get a grip. When the boardroom question is posed, 'what keeps a CEO awake at night', we need to get it all into perspective – and a global perspective, not just that of the western world. It should never be anything trivial like the success of a corporate company! It should always be how humanity can help one another... shouldn't it?

At the 2012 London Olympics, 10,500 athletes from 205 countries competed in 302 medal events at 34 venues. They used 1.8 million pieces of sporting equipment, including 8,400 shuttlecocks.

The Daily Telegraph

Nothing inspires businesspeople more than those sports men and women who train relentlessly in the quest of greatness. I have been lucky enough to hear runners Colin Jackson and Sally Gunnell and rower Ben Hunt-Davis all deliver inspirational talks on stage to share their secrets of success. Are athletes and businesspeople similar – can we humble workers compare to those great athletes? Well if you want to be successful there are some similarities in the way you must behave. You have to believe, be relentless, be tenacious, determined, let nothing stand in your way. Remain focused, driven, have a game plan to see you through the tough times and on to success. You must always believe, in unwavering terms, that you will achieve greatness and you must not let any setback slow you down.

Ben Hunt-Davis won a gold medal for rowing. He was part of a team; it was not an expected win but they had a phrase throughout their training that helped them to consider all the things they were doing leading up to the Olympics. Ben and the team asked themselves, 'Will it make the boat go faster?' and if the answer was no, they needed to stop doing it. It was simple, but when the Games opened and they all wanted to attend the opening ceremony, they asked themselves the question – they didn't go. It is like having a business mission statement and no matter how hard a decision it might be, if it won't help you achieve your goals you need to stop. You should spend 80 per cent of your time doing the things that make you money, or make your business a success. To survive and to win you need to follow these rules, no matter how hard.

Just like sportspeople, you need to create goals that inspire you, have self-belief and keep motivated, bounce back from setbacks or issues, look after the team around you, from your players to your support team, create a strong ethic and team commitment and always look to improve your approach. Do all of that with passion and excitement and whether you are a business person or an athlete – success will be yours.

> *British holidaymakers miss home after an average of 4 days*
> *and 14 hours abroad. 45 per cent take their own tea bags,*
> *but still miss that 'perfect cuppa'.*
>
> Believe in Gloucester/*The Daily Telegraph*

Bless us – we love our cups of tea and our homely comforts. This should make us a proud nation. I read this and I think of how brilliant the UK is, how amazing we are and how we love the idea of all 'being in it together'. We don't stay for the weather, for the stunning summer days – we stay for our culture, our history, our inbuilt pride of having such an amazing monarchy, a magnificent work ethic and the opportunity to work and earn money that other countries would adore. Makes you proud to be British. It makes me feel patriotic.

One of the least-known facts about the Queen's reign is that it has been accompanied by stronger economic growth than under any previous monarch, says Allister Heath in City AM, June 2012. Annual GDP growth between 1952 and 2012 averaged 2.4 per cent according to PricewaterhouseCoopers. Even Queen Victoria 'only managed 2 per cent per year' – even though Britain became the world's richest and most powerful nation when she was on the throne. The downside is that the present Queen's reign was 'bad for inflation': the retail price index has grown by 5.5 per cent per year.

We all love our homes, we just maybe struggle to love how high our taxes are, how hard it is to start a business, earn money or keep money in this country. If we could start to really address the key issues in this country we could all believe it was and is a great place all the time, irrespective of inflation and the high cost of living. To do that we need to address the simple things that affect people every day, the small ways of living that affect our state of mind or our business prospects. If we really cut through the red tape, really changed the things that mattered then maybe we would miss our homes sooner than 4 days and 14 hours... In fact maybe we would never leave!

> *54 per cent of doctors think the NHS should be allowed to refuse non-emergency treatment to patients who do not lose weight or stop smoking.*
>
> Doctors.net.uk/*The Observer*

I tend to think that if people do not look after themselves then why should they benefit from treatment that could be better used by those who really want to survive? Sadly a dear friend of mine recently lost someone very close to her – he had been diagnosed with chronic arthritis at a very young age and put on some very intrusive drugs which resulted in his lungs failing. He was 42 when they told him. Dad to two children under five and asked to wait, patiently, for a lung transplant – we waited, and waited, he got called into hospital twice but both times the lung was not for him, and tragically at 44 he died from respiratory failure, leaving a loving family behind. He never smoked; never drank (too much!); looked after himself and his family as only a real hard-working man knows how. Did he know he was going to die? Yes. Should he have jumped the queue past those waiting for the same treatment but who needed to lose weight to help aid surgery but didn't? Yes. I along with 54 per cent of doctors think you should only get out what you put in. In any commercial agreement or contract in business you award it to the best provider or supplier, to those who put in the most effort and demonstrate they want the deal more than their competitors, irrespective of the effort required and the inconvenience or trouble it may cause. That has to be fairer than the current system – if not for the individuals, then as justice for the families left behind to pick up the pieces of such devastation.

Recently the breast implant scare has raised this question: if vanity has driven an operation initially should the NHS pick up the pieces and carry out the required medical operation to remove implants that could potentially kill those infected individuals? In a harsh world you would say: if you paid for the operation initially, as it was not critical to your welfare, then you should probably be required to pay for anything that goes wrong with it down the line – freeing up the time for those individuals waiting for operations that are life or death, not just vanity. Having said that – would I want to let anyone die as a result of not being able to afford the surgery? No, of course not. The dilemma is great and I don't envy the doctors who are merely the puppets of those who make those massive judgement calls.

> *49 per cent of the public think Culture Secretary Jeremy Hunt should resign over his links with Rupert Murdoch's News Corporation. Just 16 per cent believe he should remain in his post.*
>
> ComRes/ITV News at Ten

Media is now a dirty word, with a lot of dirty secrets – we move away from accountability and credibility with every anonymous tweet or county court judgment granted to allow a 'gagging' or suppression order, to enable the restriction of information from being made public. Will it end – will we ever really believe in what we are told?

I recently got 'sold to'. I bought an advertisement in a magazine for a considerable amount of money. I was persuaded by the sales pitch and patter of the experienced salesman and I was swayed by the possibility of what could happen. I should have known better, I should never have agreed but I did. Most contracts state you cannot rely on what you are told by salespeople, the contract overrules every part of that negotiation. WHAT? Can that be right? Is that how we want to run our businesses these days?

Today it is common for contracts to contain clauses which seek to either limit or exclude liability for misrepresentation. I have had a look at several terms and conditions and there are a couple of salient clauses in them all with regard to this aspect, as follows:

2... this order is a whole agreement, containing all the terms of the agreement and it replaces any pre-contractual agreement or representations. The Authoriser admits they have not been induced to enter into this agreement by any representations made by said company or its representatives.

Unbelievable. So by signing this agreement I have made everything a salesperson has told me irrelevant!

4... the Authoriser warrants that they have formed their view as to the suitability of the advertising medium without reliance upon any representations made by said company. The parties understand that this is beyond the control of said company.

The above clauses purport to negate a company's liability. On the face of it, by signing the contract you expressly accept that there will be no guarantees, and that you were not induced to enter into the contract by any representations that were made to you. In these circumstances it will be more difficult for you to avoid the terms of the contract. To do so, you would have to establish that the above clauses are unenforceable on the basis that they fail to satisfy the test of reasonableness in the Unfair Contract Terms Act 1977.

So be warned – a good salesman can work hard for you, but a bad one can cost you dearly!

The last photocopy machine contract I was given to sign had 17 pages of small print which I read (I was stuck outside London Bridge in a train and had nothing else to do). I suddenly realized we were not guaranteed a new photocopier, despite paying for a new one; if the business felt they could provide a second-hand one that was acceptable, they would do so. I challenged the sales rep as he had clearly stipulated it would be new. He replied, 'Oh don't worry about that – it's just in there to cover us, just in case – it will probably be new'. We didn't sign it, they wouldn't remove the clause and I don't like working with people who are not up-front, honest and fair. I won't recommend them to anyone either – very short-sighted of them as a business, if they only thought one contract was at risk by not being honest.

Chapter Three
Quotes from the famous, infamous and wise

My parents brought me up to be honest, to have high moral standards and to always look to help others. I am totally agnostic so it wasn't part of a religion but it was a good way of life.

My Dad had one phrase I remember, which I believe drove me to be passionate and dedicated to what I set out to achieve – that and the fact I wanted to follow in his footsteps, which were big, not only in size but reflecting the magnitude of a great man. He always said: 'Money can't buy you the key to happiness – but if you have enough money you can afford to get a key cut!' I remember hearing it for the first time when I was young and not really understanding the true subtlety and irony of the quote; now I question if money could buy you happiness and I think the answer is no, but I also am wise enough to know that money makes the world go round. Money enables you to worry less about the things that really do weigh heavy on families and friends, the bills, the food shopping, the flat tyre, the hidden expense that means you can't afford the family holiday. If you take away all those worries simply because you have enough money then that has to help your quality of life, your focus on the daily grind and the overall contentment of those around you.

In the business world I hear quotes all the time: 'You're only as good as your last sale', 'Last one in, first one out', 'Everyone loves a lucky salesman'. However, I have collected a few from various people which I think are inspirational, motivating, amusing and poignant.

A desk is a dangerous place from which to watch the world.
John le Carré (quoted in the *San Francisco Chronicle*)

An advertising agency is 85 per cent confusion and 15 per cent commission.
Fred Allen

Never kick a man when he is down? Name me a better time.
John Cooper Clarke (quoted in the *Independent on Sunday*)

An economist is an expert who will know tomorrow why the things he predicted yesterday didn't happen today.
Laurence J Peter

To read without reflecting is like eating without digestion.
Edmund Burke

To kill an error is as good a service as, and sometimes even better than, the establishing of a new truth or fact.
Charles Darwin

If you don't know where you're going, you'll end up somewhere else.
Yogi Berra (quoted on Forbes.com)

Truth does not change because it is, or is not, believed by a majority of the people.
Giordano Bruno

And while the law of competition may be sometimes hard for the individual, it is best for the race, because it ensures the survival of the fittest in every department.
Andrew Carnegie

Meetings are indispensable when you don't want to do anything.
JK Galbraith (quoted on Financialpost.com)

As a small businessperson, you have no greater leverage than the truth.
John Greenleaf Whittier

Expecting the world to treat you fairly because you are a good person, is like expecting the bull not to attack you because you are a vegetarian.
Author Dennis Wholey (quoted in *The Sun*)

Employ your time in improving yourself by other men's writings so that you shall come easily by what others have laboured hard for.
Socrates

Though familiarity may not breed contempt, it takes the edge off admiration.
William Hazlitt (quoted in the *Buffalo News*)

A thing is not necessarily true because a man dies for it.
Oscar Wilde

Smooth seas do not make skilful sailors.
African proverb

From any single perspective, power always seems to be elsewhere.
Bertrand Russell

It's a wonderful feeling when you discover some evidence to support your beliefs.
Anonymous (quoted on Forbes.com)

A critic is a man who knows the way but can't drive the car.
Kenneth Tynan (quoted in *The Times*)

One must learn by doing the thing, for though you think you know it, you have no certainty until you try.
Aristotle

Nothing is more responsible for the good old days than a bad memory.

Franklin Pierce Adams (quoted on NewYorker.com)

The only reason some people get lost in thought is because it's unfamiliar territory!

Paul Fix, actor

Never say you know a man until you have divided an inheritance with him.

Johann Lavater, poet

You're not stuck in traffic. You are traffic.

German transport campaign

Ignorance never settles a question.

Benjamin Disraeli

Knowing your own darkness is the best method for dealing with the darkness of other people.

Carl Jung (quoted in the *Australian*)

If an idea's worth having once, it's worth having twice.

Tom Stoppard, playwright
(quoted in the *London Evening Standard*)

Always bear in mind that your own resolution to succeed is more important than any one thing.

Abraham Lincoln

If all printers were determined not to print anything till they were sure it would not offend anybody, there would be very little printed.

Benjamin Franklin

There is nothing better than a friend, unless it is a friend with chocolate.

Charles Dickens
(quoted in the *Peoria* [Illinois] *Journal*)

To follow, without halt, one aim: there's the secret of success.

Anna Pavlova

Deep down, everybody knows what 'rich' means. It means people who have slightly more than me.

Hugo Rifkind (in *The Times*)

It is possible to fail in many ways... while to succeed is possible only in one way.

Aristotle

The only difference between death and taxes is that death doesn't get worse every time congress or the government meets.

Will Rogers (quoted in *The Times*)

The greatest discovery of my generation is that a human being can alter his life by altering his attitudes of mind.

William James (1842–1910)

The single most exciting thing you encounter in government is competence, because it is so rare.

Sen. Daniel Patrick Moynihan
(quoted in the *Buffalo News*)

In the modern world of business, it is useless to be a creative original thinker unless you can also sell what you create. Management cannot be expected to recognize a good idea unless it is presented to them by a good salesman.

David M Ogilvy

The truth will set you free. But first, it will piss you off.

Gloria Steinem (quoted in *Glamour*)

My own business always bores me to death; I prefer other people's.

Oscar Wilde

If you're going to kick authority in the teeth, you might as well use two feet.

Keith Richards (quoted in the *Wall Street Journal*)

In the business world, the rear-view mirror is always clearer than the windshield.

Warren Buffett

The difference between friendship and love is how much you can hurt each other.

Ashleigh Brilliant, cartoonist
(quoted in *The Advertiser*)

The perfect bureaucrat everywhere is the man who manages to make no decisions and escape all responsibility.

Brooks Atkinson (1894–1984)

Invest in a business that even a fool can run, because some day a fool will.

Warren Buffett (quoted in *The Observer*)

Bureaucracy defends the status quo long past the time when the quo has lost its status.

Laurence J Peter (1919–1988)

If people did not sometimes do silly things, nothing intelligent would ever get done.

Ludwig Wittgenstein (in the *Buffalo News*)

Most human beings are quite likable if you don't see too much of them.

RW Lynd (quoted in the *San Francisco Chronicle*)

The consumer is not a moron; she is your wife.

David M Ogilvy

People demand freedom of speech to make up for the freedom of thought which they avoid.

Søren Kierkegaard (quoted in the *West Australian*)

To make a long story short... there's nothing like having the boss walk in.

Anonymous

Never go to bed angry. Stay up and plot revenge.

Bumper sticker

*What is a cynic? A man who knows the price of everything
and the value of nothing.*

Oscar Wilde

*There exist few modern circumstances where the removal of
the word 'strategy' from any passage containing it fails to clarify
matters, usually demonstrating the argument's circularity.*

Matthew Parris (in *The Times*)

Nothing recedes like success.

Walter Winchell, columnist

*When written in Chinese, the word crisis is composed of two
characters. One represents danger and the other represents
opportunity.*

John F Kennedy

*The only way not to think about money is to have a great
deal of it.*

Edith Wharton (quoted on RealSimple.com)

The most truthful part of a newspaper is the advertisements.

Thomas Jefferson
(quoted in the *Wall Street Journal*)

*We look on past ages with condescension, as mere preparations
for us... but what if we are a mere afterglow of them?*

J G Farrell (quoted in *The Times*)

*When we got into office, the thing that surprised me most
was to find that things were just as bad as we'd been saying
they were.*

John F Kennedy

Man finally put in charge of struggling feminist movement.

Headline in satirical magazine *The Onion*

*It is a mistake to look too far ahead. Only one link in the
chain of destiny can be handled at a time.*

Winston Churchill

This is no time for making new enemies.

Voltaire (on being asked to renounce the
devil on his deathbed)

*Accountants are the witch-doctors of the modern world and
willing to turn their hands to any kind of magic.*

British Judge Charles Eustace Harman (1894–1970)

*A meeting is an occasion when people get together, some
to say what they do not think, and others not to say what
they really do.*

Vladimir Voinovich, Russian writer

*At every party there are two kinds of people – those who want
to go home and those who don't. The trouble is they are usually
married to each other.*

Ann Landers, American agony aunt (1918–2002)

*Too bad all the people who know how to run the country are busy
driving taxi cabs and cutting hair.*

George Burns, American comedian (1896–1996)

And the most amazing quote ever – which still rings true today,
is the quote that is usually attributed to Gaius Petronius Arbiter
(c AD22–67):

*We trained hard, but it seemed that every time we were
beginning to form up into teams, we would be reorganized.
I was to learn later in life that we tend to meet any new situation
by reorganizing; and a wonderful method it can be for creating
the illusion of progress while producing confusion, inefficiency,
and demoralization.*

Chapter Four
Killer questions
Their thoughts,
your business

'You cannot please all the people all the time,' as Winston Churchill once said.

A selection of people who work for SMEs or corporate firms, from different backgrounds, varying ages and different roles, stages and successes in their careers, have been asked simple questions that shape the commercial world we all live and work within – no matter how big or small our organization, the framework remains the same – but people's views differ immensely.

One thing is certain – all of these individuals could be people you have to forge a relationship with to make your business work. But more importantly to you, most of them need to be your customers – so with such varied views, how do we please all the people all the time?

What you should remember is that when you read the questions, you will have instant views; but what if someone else makes a point that sways your view and changes your judgement, even possibly making you change your mind altogether? What if you read one of the 'killer questions' and you are certain your morals would force you to disagree – but after reading views from others you feel obliged to take that into account? Well – if you are persuaded to look at things differently, don't be disheartened and think you are not 'strong'. Being able to listen, being compassionate and accepting input is truly great; in business there is seldom a right or wrong, just a tenacious and dogged individual who wants to drive the business forward. Ruthlessness is a word only used in business in reality TV shows – not a word that should ever be used in the reality of running a company – well, not a respected, successful one anyway!

We can all learn from others, and this will help you understand your potential customer base. It will also allow you to see you cannot run a business on a few customer complaints – you must have strategic direction. The Dice Matrix Model that you will be able to complete at the end of this book will enable you to address the issues of all of your business dilemmas and requirements, not only individually but at a strategic level.

In the meantime... get to know those you work with, those you respect and those you really disagree with – it all helps the circle of networking!

This survey was conducted by myself. I selected individuals from different walks of life, people with different political allegiances and job roles, at various stages of their career or retirement and with a considerable variation in stress levels and visions. The purpose of the survey originated from a need to gain an understanding of the world we live and work in from a range of perspectives to enable me to shape a good, robust and reliable business model. The model was initially created to help deliver my own business objectives and to enable the build of a credible and reliable matrix that supported business growth and drove strategy. The Dice Matrix Model needed to be built on solid foundations from a variety of opinions, and to address the issues that were relevant and important to the masses, not just to me or my team. The answers and views from these questions were then used to help identify which questions should be put into the Dice Matrix Model to ensure we got a deliverable strategy with relevance as a final output.

The questions were written in conjunction with a panel of experts who develop psychometric and cognitive ability tests and studies. These studies enable learning, teaching and coaching courses to be written to gain the best out of people and to understand what drives a view, emotion and final decision. The questions were written in an open format, with no leading bias towards the answer. They were designed to answer the topical issues that are relevant in the world we live in today to help shape the questions we would need to ask as part of the matrix.

The survey was undertaken during May and June 2012. Everyone was e-mailed an online survey with a tight six-week period in which to respond to ensure the economic and environmental situations were the same for all contributions. Individuals completed the survey knowing only I would be reading the answers and they would not be attributed to them once published – so they were asked to be very honest, to give the response they genuinely believed and not what they thought society would 'want' them to feel.

No structure was given as to how they should answer the questions; they did not have to respond to all of the questions or remain consistent if they felt differently about their views from question to question. These answers have all helped shape the questions for the Dice Matrix Model, ensuring the most relevant output possible.

Whose business is it!?

1   Should a business be allowed to use the 'offshore' rule and 'get away' with not paying the rate of UK tax required due to a spurious headquarters in a tax haven?

Morally no, but what happens if you start to go after the massive global companies that employ in Britain and do pay tax here, even if they could and possibly should be paying more? Be careful what you wish for!

GH, drainage cleaner, male,
37, honours degree, privately educated

No. Full tax should be paid on all profit made from trading in the UK no matter where the company is based. The use of offshore tax havens should be made illegal.

JP, retired civil servant, 69, male, first class
honours degree in engineering

I don't believe that if a company is making genuine profit from activities in the UK but is domiciled in Ireland (for instance) that it should be able to not pay the relevant taxes for that privilege. The idea of tax havens does not offend me as each country has the ability to set its tax rates for internal and external residences and that is what gives each country the ability to be competitive; however, a company that is resident in one country but makes profit mainly from business generated in the UK should be paying UK tax rates.

PS, city stockbroker, 34, male, privately educated

I did not understand this – but on consultation with the ceramic artist I have some lessons with (ie a small business person) I report her comment: 'If it is legal to use the offshore rule then you can't accuse someone of "getting away with it". If it is legal it is therefore OK'.

My comment: there seems to be confusion here between what is legal and what is ethical.

JC, retired religious education teacher,
69, female, public sector

This is a tough question to answer, asking a question of business ethics over morality. Personally, I believe that 'loopholes' like these should be closed and British companies should pay the full rate of tax as other British companies who do not have access to funds to employ the Big Four accountancy firms to make them more 'tax efficient'. I should acknowledge that this is a very Utopian vision and I realize that British companies would not acquiesce to such a requirement all the while their international competitors do not have the same requirements. Fundamentally I believe in fair play and this is why I believe that business and its shareholders have a responsibility for doing the right thing for the regions they work in. Once again though, a multinational would then move HQ to another region it works in which perhaps has a more tax friendly approach.

CK, sales manager (corporate firm),
45, male, state education (left school at 16)

I think this depends on the size of the business. If it is a tiny enterprise, there are those that would consider this selfish on the part of the owner. However, if this was a large business, one has to look at the workforce size and the income this generates for the exchequer. Example: Tyco [International Ltd].

HS, British diplomatic community member,
45, male, lives in Belgium

If a business is trading in the UK it should have to pay the same level of taxes as businesses whose main business address is a UK address. UK businesses should be supporting our economy overall although I understand how attractive the tax loophole is for those who are making huge profits... after all why should they want to give so much away to the taxman. However, if any of their employees and their families are living in the UK and receiving the benefits of being a UK citizen then they should be paying their portion of tax. If the company ceases trading it will be companies that are trading in the proper way that will support those that are out of work and still living on British soil. What I don't understand is why there are any safe tax havens on soil that is considered British?!? Surely we should all be governed by the same working laws regardless of location if the soil is considered British?

SR, single mum/self-employed
business owner, 36, female

*If the utilization of tax havens is legal, then any business
should be allowed to benefit therefrom. It is the responsibility
of government to close loopholes if they consider that to be the
right course of action.*

MP, chairman of top FTSE
100 international business, 65, male

*No – I believe that if you trade within a country you should abide
by their tax rules and regulations. I find it bemusing that a certain
large retail supermarket chain can claim they are based 'offshore'
and pay little or no tax into the UK system. Companies benefiting
from the 'offshore' potential loophole are only those major players
who should not benefit from playing the system but should be on the
same level playing field as any other UK business. By turning a blind
eye to this abuse it not only harms the potential growth of any new
business, but it over-taxes the average SME and individual to make
up the shortfall deficit. I believe the government is only too quick
to close any loophole that could help private individuals but they
choose to turn a blind eye to their larger 'partners' and allies when it
comes to corporate tax. I fully understand the need to retain money
to input and invest back into a business to allow it to grow, but in
my opinion all businesses, irrespective of size, should be playing to
the same rules, and those rules are those of HMRC.*

SC, company director, 37, female,
married with two children

2   **Should both corporate and SMEs have the same responsibility for
maternity leave and pension contribution?**

*Yes. An individual should not suffer just because he/she works
for an SME. Likewise a corporate should not 'subsidize' an SME
in this respect, which would effectively be the outcome if outside
assistance were to be given to SMEs.*

MP, chairman of top FTSE
100 international business, 65, male

The responsibility for maternity leave has become far too demanding for all companies but particularly for small companies. There are many small employers who have been so stung by maternity provision that they will no longer consider employing women of child-bearing age. The requirement for small companies should be reconsidered. Pension is different and it is not unreasonable for the requirement to be the same for all companies. I believe that the government should rationalize the whole pension provision and amalgamate a basic pension provision with the state pension and that provision should be enhanced by national insurance payments. It would then be up to the individual whether they make further provision or not.

JP, retired civil servant, 69, male, first class
honours degree in engineering

Certainly not. Our global competitors must chuckle at the naïve approach of the European Union that has of course filtered down by regulation to Great Britain. China, India and other developing (or one could argue that they are now developed) economies in their own right would never give workers such ludicrous rights. Even the USA, one of our direct competitors in the western, developed world is more business friendly, even with a quasi-socialist leader in Obama. I have heard many a small business leader say to me, 'I'd never employ a woman, they get pregnant and I'm screwed'. However, the production line of children is essential; otherwise there is no future for the economy and the country. So what does an SME or micro business do? There should be a minimum maternity leave, say 60 per cent lower than a corporate, big beast would have to provide. When a contract was offered, the SME/micro could put forward the contract and its reasons for offering only 50 per cent of the maternity cover offered by larger organizations. The same is even more applicable to holiday entitlement. In these über-tough economic times, SMEs and micro businesses simply cannot afford to allow 28 days' holiday a year. My colleagues and I average around five to seven days a year and as we look to expand and take on more staff we need to be able to say to potential new recruits that their limit is 10 days. If circumstances change we will consider increasing that to 15 and so on. Times are tough; hard graft required and small businesses cannot be choked by social working regulation that has been drafted in a one-size-fits-all manner. A direct consequence of this is that SMEs and micro businesses will be tempted to hire 'casual', dare I say cash-in-hand employees, not to avoid the national insurance contributions, but simply to not have to abide by working benefits and regulations. We are not living in a Dickensian era where the worker is spending 18 hours a day in a match factory, but legislators need to wake up and understand the restrictions that social working laws place upon the small business. If its owners can work 18-hour days and take five days holiday a year and they are offering employment as the job queues lengthen, then so can the employee. This isn't the boom times of pre-2008, so in conclusion, sit on benefit of £65 a week or earn £500 a week, but when you do get your five days in the sun, make sure you enjoy them!

GH, drainage cleaner, male, 37,

honours degree, privately educated

To this question I would answer no. In principle this should be the case but from my knowledge of SMEs there is not the funding to make this a practical agreement. I certainly believe bigger companies should make this a benefit and it should be advertised as such when they recruit, as very much being a benefit for working for company A. With regards to SMEs and maternity leave, government does its bit in this area and I would not ask for more money to make this achievable. It might be a rather harsh viewpoint but prospective parents should weigh these decisions up at the time. Statutory maternity leave for example should not be stretched to encourage more couples to conceive. This is a lifestyle decision and should be made knowing that a finite amount of money will be paid out over the course of a six-month period.

With regards to SMEs and pension contribution, I again feel that this is too prohibitive financially (taking the general consensus of an SME being under 250 employees).

CK, sales manager (corporate firm), 45, male,
state education (left school at 16)

Yes, in short if anyone looks to start an SME they do so knowing they will not be sharing a proportion of profits with shareholders or board members. SMEs are vital in the country to ensure growth but to attract good employees to this area of business they need to pull their weight and protect their employees otherwise who would want to work for an SME when they can work for a larger company and receive many benefits which equate to a higher rate of pay.

SR, single mum/self-employed business
owner, 36, female

SMEs should not have the same responsibility for pension contributions in my opinion as that sort of burden is counter-productive for a business that is trying to grow or establish itself... every penny counts. I believe that maternity rights in the UK are set out fairly as it stands and that it would harm the ability of SMEs to hire the right people if they did not have the requirement to offer maternity rates.

PS, city stockbroker, 34, male,
privately educated

Working for an SME should be an attractive option, but the pressure on the SME during maternity puts a greater pressure on it. A form of subsidy should be considered so that the leave does not become a major hindrance during the leave time. Should a subsidy be available, then yes an SME should have the same responsibility.

HS, British diplomatic community member,
45, male, lives in Belgium

*This is a tough question for me. I have had two children
and taken maternity leave twice; both times I only took six
months, driven by the fact I could not afford to take more
time off and the honest fact I love working. I don't feel
ashamed to say I am a better mother when I work and have
something beyond the children in my life. I did feel a little
guilty when I took maternity leave but I had worked for the
corporate company for 13 years when I took the six months
off so I felt I had paid my time into the pot to allow this time
off 'guilt' free. However, I now own an SME and we would
seriously struggle to pay someone for a long period of time
whilst they had a baby, plus we would need to replace said
member of staff which would be an additional cost. I do
understand the importance of being able to have a baby without
being penalized by the fact you work for an SME – so if honest,
I think yes, SMEs should have the same obligations to pay
maternity, and the employee should be made to feel like it is not
an issue – after all having children and reproducing is one of the
most important aspects of our being.*

SC, company director, 37, female,
married with two children

*My adviser – the ceramic artist and her students that I got
input from – says SMEs cannot possibly have the same
responsibilities. If you only have yourself and employ one
employee you can't afford to cover that one person. Anyone
who is of child-bearing age has to take their own responsibility
for their work and pregnancy – and has to think ahead that if
they work for a small company it won't be able to offer all the
perks a bigger one can. (And probably won't employ you anyway
if they suspect you will go off to have a baby. Women are caught
here by their biology.)*

JC, retired religious education teacher,
69, female, public sector

3   Should we have allowed our utilities companies to be bought by corporate companies; does it matter that most of them are not British?

Free markets imply that all is for sale to the highest bidder.
Should it be allowed? Yes and no. My reasoning is as follows.
A company such as GDF SUEZ (French utility) has taken over the
Belgian energy network and has raised prices in Belgium to the
detriment of the local consumer in order to artificially lower prices
in its home market, along with other competitive markets, and to
fund investment abroad. There should be some sort of safeguard
in place to stop this geo-political manoeuvring. Does it matter
that the company is not British? No I don't think so.

HS, British diplomatic community member,
45, male, lives in Belgium

NEVER! It matters enormously that our utilities providers have
been purchased by overseas companies. I admire the way that a
lot of European countries manage who can and can't invest in
their home utilities companies and reject offers to purchase their
blue-chip companies from overseas; I feel that the country would
be doing far better had we been a little nationalist. This country
was never in a stronger position than when our engineering and
manufacturing sectors were thriving.

PS, city stockbroker, 34, male,
privately educated

Utility companies should ideally be government-owned so they are
properly regulated and offer good value for money to consumers.
In an ideal world these would be operated on a non-profit basis
as rising costs in all utilities have such a high impact on those
that are pensioned or not working. Everyone should be entitled
to warmth and electricity regardless of their income. If you ask
most people, I am sure they would prefer to pay a higher rate
of tax but have their utilities provided in the same way that we

*pay for the NHS. Why are commercial companies ruling whether
those who have worked all their lives are no longer able to afford
to turn on their heaters in the winter for fear of a huge gas bill?
If it is not possible to retain utilities under government rule there
should at least be the provision that companies buying the rights
to sell utilities have to set guidelines on profit levels that can
obtain within this industry/market. Profits should not be the main
focus of utility providers. Whether the owning company should
be British would not be important if rules pertaining to profit
margins were enforced as the companies would be working for the
public interest regardless of the nationality of the owning body.*

SR, single mum/self-employed business
owner, 36, female

*No, we should never have privatized our utilities. There are certain
essential services that should be owned by the people as a whole and
controlled by their elected politicians for the benefit of the country.
Competition in some services is so artificial or even non-existent that
to say privatization was beneficial because it introduced competition
is nonsense. True, there was room for efficiency improvements in
the nationalized industries, but if only a fraction of the effort and
non-productive marketing etc had been put into the nationalized
industries they would be serving the country so much better than the
assorted private companies, many now foreign-owned without our
best interests their concern, just their profit.*

*Consider water: there is no choice or competition and prices
have rocketed; our latest bill showed that 41 per cent of the cost
of water was in financing capital expenditure, so even with the
high bills we are not paying our way but are again mortgaging
the future for the next generation to pay. Consider the railways
where the subsidies from the tax payer are now considerably
higher in real terms than they were when it was a nationalized
company. It is a fundamental of good business not to split
responsibility for providing a service. Consider electricity where
it is easy to forget how effective it was as a nationalized industry*

*– it standardized our supplies, as before nationalization there
were different voltages (some AC, some DC) and all too
often when you moved you had to change all your electrical
equipment to suit the new supplier. It built the power stations
and distribution network to cater for a doubling in capacity every
ten years, making a profit for the government in the process,
whereas the privatized companies are struggling to maintain the
existing capacity and unless they get considerable help from the
government will fail to do so. It also made us a world leader in
nuclear power, a lead we have since squandered and are now
dependent on foreign companies.*

*We now have energy policies primarily determined by the
short-term interest of private companies. An example of this
was the rush to use gas to generate electricity at an efficiency
of about 40 per cent, using up much of the North Sea reserves
instead of preserving them for gas-fired boilers in homes and
businesses where it could be utilised at 90 per cent efficiency.
It is also a widely held fallacy that gas power stations produce
less greenhouse gases than coal-fired stations when considering
the total picture. Competition is again meaningless, for you switch
to a cheaper supplier only for their price to change within a couple
of months; changing can be very frustrating and consider the
millions of non-productive hours annually wasted in this process.
It surely cannot be logical to buy electricity from a Scottish
company who has to use your local company to deliver it to you,
and even less logical to buy your gas from a company whose core
business is electrical distribution. We now have endless quangos
that make no contribution to the productivity of the nation and
merely produce red tape and unnecessary regulations.*

*That many of our utilities are owned by foreign companies
is an absolute disaster and all the talk of us being a global
marketplace and thus it doesn't matter is just nonsense – which
regrettably I believe we will discover in the not too distant future.*

JP, retired civil servant, 69, male, first class
honours degree in engineering

*In short, yes and no. In today's globalized economy I see no
problem with foreign ownership of these utility companies. I would
assume that as these are regulated industries in the UK, there are
safeguards built in to any licence, with regards to the provision of
services and tariffs charged, so the consumer is protected.*

CK, sales manager (corporate firm), 45, male,

state education (left school at 16)

*We either have a free climate for foreign investment or not.
I do not think that utilities are sufficiently sensitive to protect
them from overseas acquisition. If this were to be done, it would
probably re-introduce inefficiencies and costs to the consumer
would increase. If there is a problem at any time, then that can
be dealt with by the government of the day.*

MP, chairman of top FTSE 100 international business, 65, male

*No – it saddens me greatly that we came from being such a
great country to one of 'selling off the silver'. We appear to have
mortgaged everything we could up to the hilt! I think the essence
of privatization was initially a potentially good idea but now we
have nothing left, we manufacture nothing and as a country, we
appear to have nothing we can be proud of. Our utilities are all
owned by corporate companies, most based overseas and when
profit is made it does not go to the UK bottom line, it goes to
France or Germany. Other countries insisted that any buy-out
should be kept insular and within their own countries – I fear
we should have done the same to ensure any required investment
occurs correctly and under UK legislation. If we had maintained
the utilities the UK would benefit when growth occurs. We will all
always need water, electricity and gas – so why sell it!*

SC, company director, 37, female,

married with two children

*I have always believed that the private sector beats the public
sector nine times out of ten. I believe that the state should be*

responsible for the following: defence, policing, prisons, courts, foreign affairs and roads. Everything else should be in the hands of the individual and the private sector. However it appears, although the media may exaggerate the difference, that the charges levied in the UK by French- and German-owned utility companies are greater if not far greater than in their 'native' countries. Energy prices alone in this country are unsustainable. Perhaps we should re-open our deep coal mines?

GH, drainage cleaner, male, 37, honours degree, privately educated

All of the ceramics group felt it is wrong somehow to be owned by non-British companies – but no solid reasons could be given, unless there is a worry about the political situation of the foreign country and its finances.

JC, retired religious education teacher, 69, female, public sector

4 **How would you make large corporate companies more ethical; do they need it, and do we have the right?**

I think large and even small companies should be more ethical and I believe government can pass certain laws to help. I certainly think the John Lewis model is a good one to copy; the difficulty is how to persuade or even force companies to follow it. I think limiting the ratio of the highest earner to the lowest earner to, say, 20 would help and perhaps making it a requirement that at least 50 per cent of a company's shares must be owned by people working for the company and that no individual or organization should be allowed to hold more than say 5 per cent in the case of large companies. Companies that have grown to be successful in this country and then decide to manufacture or base overseas should face heavy penalties.

JP, retired civil servant, 69, male, first class honours degree in engineering

Ethics is something that is looked at by the consumer with scepticism. We tend to base ethics on Western society values and the 'sleep sound at night' mentality. Emerging economies offer cheap capital and despite working conditions not being constrained by the same legislation, the local workforce are 'looked after' in comparison to what was on offer before. It is due to Western-style consumerism and the prices that we are willing to pay, that a company such as Apple or Samsung will seek cheap labour to maximize profits and shareholder returns. In the event of an ethical outcry, the margins available allow room for improvements and a good PR exercise.

HS, British diplomatic community member,
45, male, lives in Belgium

Large corporate companies have an obligation to be ethical and I think that this feeds through the layers of management within that company. Thus the board have a crucial role to play in setting out a company's ethics! As such, a board of directors should be very carefully selected so that a diverse set of individuals preside; this diversity should keep a company on the straight and narrow. Public limited companies have a shareholder base that has a responsibility to keep the board in check and manage out of the business any executives that no longer work to the ethics of that company; all too often shareholders are not bold enough to step in and take action if they see a company making poor decisions! As a group the government, in my mind, only has the right to place sanctions on companies that break laws or where the state has a shareholding that warrants those sanctions. Indirectly the specific regulators are government agencies and they should be given the ability to sanction a company if ethics seem to be drifting!

PS, city stockbroker, 34, male,
privately educated

Ethical? The incoming Labour government in 1997 thought they could have an 'ethical' foreign policy and Robin Cook the new

*foreign secretary tried to champion this. Naïve in the extreme.
What is ethical? This is such a broad and sweeping subject
that can encompass almost all aspects of corporate activity.
BP in the Gulf of Mexico were responding to desire for cheap
US pump prices and drilling deeper than ever and in hazardous
conditions; the result, environmental disaster and Britain's biggest
corporate behemoth nearly destroyed. So should BP just focus on
green and renewable energy? Of course not. Do you trade with
China? Their human rights record is atrocious. Of course you do
or others will. Bismarck would say 'Realpolitik'. Big business is
a treacherous and dog-eat-dog world. Ethical equates to being
handicapped and no more sales of jet fighters to Saudi Arabia.
In short, no.*

GH, drainage cleaner, male,
37, honours degree, privately educated

*It's a massive generalization to say that all large companies are
not ethical but I truly believe there is more that the majority can
do in this area. I believe the way forward for this kind of action
must come from shareholder pressure, as they are the ones who
have the stake in the company and more and more, we see that
active shareholders can and do hold executive teams to account.
Do we have the right? By we, I answer as the shareholder and yes
we do have that right and I think it's an implicit right.*

CK, sales manager (corporate firm),
45, male, state education (left school at 16)

*Any large corporate company should ideally work to ethical
guidelines but this is unrealistic to manage and govern due to
the scale of the companies. Perhaps there should be better
incentives for companies to work ethically. If they are offering
better support and packages to their employees or sourcing
products and services from companies that have received a
'gold star' they should receive a cash-back incentive direct to
shareholders to reflect the ethical status of the corporation.*

This would ensure that shareholders and board members push for the corporation to be ethical in their approach if there is a financial benefit to the decision makers. I know I would be pushing for products to be ethically sourced if the government was to offer a cash incentive that was profit-related direct into my pocket. The urge to go for cost effectiveness over ethics is too strong in the current economic climate.

SR, single mum/self-employed business
owner, 36, female

I felt this to be an unclear question. What is meant by ethical? Environmentally? Working conditions of employees? Equality in the workforce? The stuff being made – weapons? Taking jobs from other companies by undercutting them? Getting stuff made by very poor people in poor countries on low wages? The term 'ethical' is so broad a term that as it is used in this question it is meaningless. My view is that: assuming that an agreement is reached as to what is meant by ethical in relation to a particular company, then clearly every company and every person should be ethical. Just as every company should be legal. 'Do they need it?' Surely everyone needs to consider their own moral values and judgements and apply their decisions to their work. 'Do we have a right?' Everyone has the right to hold their own moral position and a duty to put their morals into action – by, for example, not working for a company they disapprove of (and then they have the additional moral/ethical challenge to decide whether it is better for their family to have an unemployed father/mother or a parent who is working for a company s/he is uncomfortable with). No easy answers. If the question 'do we have a right?' means 'does the government have the right' the answer is that all government should oversee the behaviour of companies as to their legality and their practices. Ethical issues are very hard for a government to legislate on, but they should try.

JC, retired religious education teacher,
69, female, public sector

I believe there are different levels of ethical. Should a company use illegal methods to make a gain? No, certainly not. Should they abide by the rules and regulations? Yes. But should the self-appointed industry bodies and quasars [government-funded regulatory bodies] be allowed to dictate what happens to a business and its boardroom judgement calls? No, they should in my mind have no power at all. It is crazy that we as a country spend so much money on funding the bodies that run the various sectors of business fairly. I remember the good old days when you could ring 192 to get a directory number from BT – you knew what it would cost, you knew the number would be correct, you knew if it did not work you would be refunded with no questions asked. Now, thanks to competition law and quasars/quangos I can call a variety of different companies, I have no idea what anything costs, no idea if the connection will work and no idea if I will get a refund if the right number is not given. This was all carried out under the guise of help for the end-user, but commercial choice is not necessary in some cases or in fact helpful to the end-user. A few months ago I wanted to move my gas meter after some serious renovation to our home. We use one electric company to purchase our gas; after many phone calls, many letters and many frustrated groans from myself we discovered that although we had a 'choice' to move a meter we had to use SGN 'Southern Gas Network' (or, as the workmen told me they called it, 'Still Going Nowhere') who had a fixed cost, certain rules and regulations and no available time slot for many months. Could we use anyone else? No. Could we get an independent person to carry out this work? No. Did having a 'choice' enable us to negotiate prices, or choose a supplier? No. I miss the simple days!

SC, company director, 37, female,
married with two children

Large corporates should not be forced to be any more ethical than others. Listed companies do however produce very detailed reports of their policies for social responsibilities and these are usually compliant with the 'Code'. The system works quite well at the moment and further legislation, rather than voluntary disclosure, would be counter-productive. If 'we' are not a customer or shareholder in the large corporate, then we should not have the 'right' to interfere. Organizations such as Fairtrade and Rainforest Alliance can be much more effective than general legislation.

MP, chairman of top FTSE
100 international business, 65, male

5   **Does the government have the right to sanction pay in publicly owned (listed/private) companies?**

Definitely not. This is a matter for the shareholders and independent non-executive directors.

MP, chairman of top FTSE
100 international business, 65, male

I believe that government can have no place in setting the pay guidelines for any publicly owned company. There are far too many areas where government overreaches its remit, pandering to the public issue of that day. It is for shareholders to hold boards to account on these such issues.

CK, sales manager (corporate firm),
45, male, state education (left school at 16)

Not only do they not have the right, they should not have the power. Government can and will change potentially every four years, they have short-term goals, short-term visions and should never be allowed to set parameters within private businesses. They would only look to the quick win of their government term and not the long-term success of the country or the private business. A lot of fuss is made about what people earn in bonuses and the like – I agree we have got out of control in some pay

structures, but as long as a footballer can earn over £200,000
a week and a nurse gets no more than minimum wage despite
working for the government, I believe the less government gets
involved the better.

SC, company director, 37, female,
married with two children

I think as an aside it would be good to clarify what 'public'
means: does it mean the public as a whole or just certain members
of the public? After all public schools are in fact private schools.
If we consider companies owned by individuals and shareholders
then the government, apart from setting overall criteria like
minimum wages, can and should do little to influence pay.
If it doesn't like certain trends then taxation is its best weapon.

JP, retired civil servant, 69, male,
first class honours degree in engineering

The government should produce enforceable guidelines that
are realistic for all companies to work with. This would not
necessarily be a one-fits-all solution but to have an audit of each
business to determine the level it can reasonably afford would
give some structure to pay scales and safeguard employees at the
same time. The idea of the government working as a 'big brother'
is not great but there are many companies working inscrutably at
the moment and if there was a sliding scale that worked in line
with company profits it would stop certain companies trading
where they are not looking after their employees' interests. The
idea of restricting the big bonus culture we live in at the moment
is also very appealing but much harder to enforce. I understand
that there are a number of talented individuals working within
the banking industry where they receive a lower basic salary than
their counterparts would receive but balance it out with bonuses
based on results. There should be guidelines on how these bonuses
are paid. I don't disagree with bonuses being paid but it should
reflect good and solid decisions made rather than rewarding

*high-risk moves by certain individuals. To be fair, those in the
position of taking risks have created profits within the UK
economy that in past years, when we have all benefited from
economic growth, has meant more cash in our pockets. In
addition if these levels of bonuses are paid within one industry
then it should follow suit that the same levels of bonuses should
be paid in other sectors, otherwise why would anyone wish to go
into an industry without the opportunity to earn bonuses?*

SR, single mum/self-employed business
owner, 36, female

NO.

HS, British diplomatic community member,
45, male, lives in Belgium

*No, I don't believe that the government has the right to sanction
pay in a private company. Private companies are just that and
should not answer to anyone external; they pay their taxes to the
country (hopefully) and should be able to pay their staff what
they deem fair! Listed companies have shareholders that vote
each year on director positions and those appointed to the board
should manage the company's pay structure. The government
recently indicated that shareholders would be given a mandatory
vote on executives' pay and this should be implemented
as soon as possible; if executive pay is regulated by the owners
of a business then the correct pay schemes will filter down the
ranks of that company.*

PS, city stockbroker, 34, male,
privately educated

*Never. Capitalism has lost its way, but start interfering and what
do you create? They have effectively sanctioned pay in these
companies by interfering with a 'banker's tax' that affects all
people regulated by the FSA, from insurance broker to commodity
broker. Why? They are not bankers and why should it apply*

to non-state (majority-owned such as RBS) banks? Why not a
footballer's tax?

GH, drainage cleaner, male,
37, honours degree, privately educated

I said Yes, as the people democratically elect a government and
then we have to trust it to run the companies properly – including
controlling its pay. However in my ceramics group most people
thought my answer was far too much like life under communism
and they were for free enterprise: let everyone try to get as much
pay as they can and let the companies get away with paying
a little as they can.

JC, retired religious education teacher,
69, female, public sector

6   What are your views on the litigious society we now live in;
do you worry about being sued as a business?

Continual litigation is a growing concern. Courts should
be given the responsibility of throwing out spurious claims
and strongly sanctioning those that seek to benefit therefrom.
Ambulance chasing and associated strategies should be banned.

MP, chairman of top FTSE
100 international business, 65, male

Society has become far too litigious and a greedy legal
profession must take much of the blame for this. Many
prospective actions should be thrown out right at the start.
Too many people have accidents due to their own negligence or
stupidity and sue a business that could not reasonably be held
liable. Should somebody who slips on a floor get compensation
when everyone else has taken care and not slipped? I have long
thought the NHS could save a lot of money and be far more
efficient if it was not possible to sue them; the service is free,
you use it at your risk. Perhaps there could be an independent

commission to award compensation in extreme cases of negligence. I think most people worry about being sued and spend a lot insuring against the possibility. Should you clear snow from the pavement outside your house? Should you fence off lakes in case trespassers drown? Should you leave a hazard in your house that a burglar might not see in the dark? I think the real problem stems from the legal profession itself. Consider the case of Dales Farm. It was a clear cut case of infringing planning law and should have been settled with a 10-minute court hearing with no right of appeal. Instead it was only resolved after 10 years with considerable legal costs and acrimony. The only ones to gain from this were the lawyers. The council were faced with huge costs and ironically the travellers were not well served as the houses they had built were in the end demolished. The whole episode is an indictment of our legal system.

JP, retired civil servant, 69, male,
first class honours degree in engineering

I truly believe that the litigious nature in the UK is driving down this country's effectiveness for enterprise as businesses become paralyzed by fear of risk. As a business my own employers are relentlessly keen on safety and protecting members of the public on our sites. The wider issue around this matter is the moral decay that has accelerated with the introduction of no-win, no-fee legal companies. It is creating a society whereby people abdicate responsibility for their own personal safety, in favour of it always being someone else's fault/responsibility. It was recently announced that the UK is the 'whiplash capital' of Europe. Something that should embarrass each and every one of us.

CK, sales manager (corporate firm),
45, male, state education (left school at 16)

Dear God, can we possibly worry about getting sued and still get out of bed and work a full day... every company must now worry about our litigious society. However, if you have created and run a business you are the type of individual who is not fearful of these challenges but accepts them and works with good insurances to try and safeguard the business. You cannot walk outside your front door without someone trying to sue someone else because they feel they have received anything from a bad meal to bad service... it's ridiculous and not at all 'British'. We are quickly catching on to the American way of viewing litigation as a tool to receive money if we feel we have been mistreated, but as with many areas of life, I believe this is a generational thing that will go full circle and the next generation will have grown bored with the challenge and it will fade out.

SR, single mum/self-employed
business owner, 36, female

Damn disgrace. I do not worry because if it happens it happens, rather like a terrorist bomb on the underground. If it happens, c'est la vie. What I will say is that the tribunal system must change. The following example will suffice. 60-year-old white male who has worked for the same company for 44 years who goes to tribunal for unfair or constructive dismissal is limited to a £75,000 maximum award. Person who has been at a company for six months and sues for religious, sexual, racial or disability discrimination: award unlimited if proven. Absolute lunacy.

GH, drainage cleaner, male, 37,
honours degree, privately educated

Everyone said there is far too much running to the law, never taking personal responsibility or taking the blame. Small companies cannot be expected to pay huge sums in compensation. So long as all sensible precautions have been made to protect their employees the company has done its best and the employees have to be responsible for any accidents they have caused to themselves or others.

JC, retired religious education teacher,
69, female, public sector

When I set up my SME I was told I would need insurance,
but I had no idea what this would need to cover – the fact that
if something we sold 'poisoned' any one we would need to
be covered, if it arrived broken and someone hurt themselves
we would need to be covered, if the delivery man dropped it
on the carpet – we would need to be covered. If we missed a
deadline delivery date – you guessed it: cover! At the same time
I was selling a property which apparently needed a few special
indemnity insurance policies, one in case the house was placed
near a church that had the right to ask under covenant for
finances to help do any maintenance work, a second in case it
was near a flood plain, and a third insurance cover of a special
policy to safeguard against radon gas being in the ground –
because nothing helps radon gas disappear more than an
insurance indemnity! I am sure at some point someone will
take legal action against my small business – I only hope we
have the right policy!

SC, company director, 37, female,
married with two children

This is one of the worst aspects of living in this country currently!
The 'no-win, no-fee' culture is one that promotes blame rather
than responsibility and is a real problem for businesses. The
amount of time and money spent on protecting a business from
the threat of legal action is concerning and I firmly believe that
if this threat were taken away, or at least lessened, we would see
the recovery gather pace!

PS, city stockbroker, 34, male,
privately educated

7   **Is the 50 per cent tax bracket penalizing the economy drivers or is**
it fair to tax higher earners?

Tax is paid for the benefit of all citizens. The government
provides a service. It is not the government's responsibility to

'penalize' high earners. Logically speaking each individual
should pay the same percentage of tax on their earnings. If that
rate were for example 25 per cent then someone with a salary
of say £50,000 would pay tax of £12,500 and someone earning
£100,000 would pay tax of £25,000 for the same service from
government, ie twice the amount. Even this seems unfair and
any higher rate tax is, by its nature, counter-productive to the
individual and thereby, the country. A higher rate of tax is
therefore only the result of envy. A 50 per cent rate was rightly
deemed to be counter-productive and will be reduced to
45 per cent. This is not nearly low enough. Experience shows
that low-taxed countries are usually more successful and
dynamic than those that are higher-taxed.

MP, chairman of top FTSE
100 international business, 65, male

The 50 per cent tax bracket is currently penalizing those
that are driving the economy and I believe that this country
is making itself less appealing to those that earn that amount
of money. Again we as a country need to be looking to be as
competitive as possible and I feel that the 40 per cent bracket
was sufficient. Most of those that fall into that bracket are
paying taxes post-income tax on purchases they make and
I feel the government would do well to think of how much
they would take in earnings if those on 50 per cent were freed
to spend again. There are other proposals that I believe make
sense like taxing the super-rich non-domiciles that manage to
keep most of their money offshore; a minimum tax payment
would address tax loopholes and not punish those that happily
pay the top rate each year.

PS, city stockbroker, 34, male,
privately educated

Why tax high earners more just because they have (in most
instances) worked hard to achieve well in life? We should

recognize these individuals as a rare talent and reward them for the sacrifices they have no doubt had to make in their personal lives to reach the level they have. There is not an easy answer to how do you set tax levels... maybe it should go on the age of earners... give those that have just started working a tax break so they can save and get on the housing ladder and those that have been working longer pay a sliding scale of tax depending on age. How do you make it fair? No one seems to have the answer to this but personally the 50 per cent tax bracket is no incentive for people to work harder and longer if they feel the government is penalizing them. After all whether you earn £15,000 a year or £150,000 you receive the same benefits if you are made unemployed or need medical care. High earners should not be required to shore up the rest of the UK!

SR, single mum/self-employed business
owner, 36, female

An unclear question. Is this about petrol tax and driving or about tax in general? If it is about tax in general: in discussion there was no agreement on this. It was felt that a balance was needed. If you taxed high earners too much they might be ready to remove their money to other countries, but on the other hand if anyone can afford to pay a lot of tax they should pay. High earners are not necessarily driving the economy. Low-paid workers are just as vital. My view: you have to question what tax is for. You have to say: the country needs medical care, education, roads and transport etc, and so you tax everyone enough to pay only for these necessities. And if not enough money is raised, the people must be consulted and invited to pay all they can to cover these costs. Using percentages as a base for fixing tax is never fair because one per cent of a little is a lot less than one per cent of a lot, but the people who only have a little and lose some of that find it far harder to bear than people with a lot who lose a lot. Just as there is a fixed minimum wage, people could/should

*consider what is meant by a fair maximum wage. It would be
an interesting debate.*

JC, retired religious education teacher,
69, female, public sector

*I'm not personally affected by this tax bracket so my thoughts
should be seen in that context. However, I do not believe that the
50 per cent rate is punishing the economy drivers and I think it is
incumbent on the higher earners to contribute more to the country.
However, I also believe that the 50 per cent rate should be raised
from £150,000 pa to a figure nearer the £200,000 mark.*

CK, sales manager (corporate firm), 45, male,
state education (left school at 16)

*I am lucky enough to pay this rate – and so I should, I only wish
those taking the money were spending it better. If you earn well
you pay tax, the more you earn the more you should contribute.
Enough said.*

SC, company director, 37, female,
married with two children

*The argument here is hard. Very difficult to explain to the masses
that someone earning over £150,000 cannot or should not pay
50 per cent and therefore this becomes a political hotcake. What
is an economy driver? An employed banker or lawyer earning
£250,000? A council chief exec earning £220,000? Or the business
owner who is earning £142,000 and wants to see that increase by
£40,000 each year as his company expands and grows. I would
say the last example and perhaps then that business owner should
only pay 40 per cent, but then this opens up another can of worms.
Easily dealt with, as I have stated: reduce state spending to the core
areas of state responsibility in Question 3 and then everybody rich
and poor can have their tax rate reduced to 10p in the pound.*

GH, drainage cleaner, male, 37,
honours degree, privately educated

*The 50 per cent tax bracket isn't penalizing the economy
drivers although there are those who believe it doesn't
bring in any more tax as the higher rate acts as an incentive
to find ways round paying the higher tax. The answer here
is to stop those tax-avoiding schemes. What isn't fair is for
very high earners to pay at a rate lower than the comparatively
low earner.*

JP, retired civil servant, 69, male,
first class honours degree in engineering

*As with any fiscal policy, it depends on where the ceilings are
fixed. The decision must not be political and must aim to be
both coherent and fair. Will it bring revenue to the exchequer in
a way that will make an impact? Perhaps a better answer is to
progressively raise the lower income tax level.*

HS, British diplomatic community member,
45, male, lives in Belgium

8   **Does more legislation and legal paperwork exist year on year;
does it stop you doing the day job?**

*It doesn't affect me directly; however, the hurdles that people
have to go through to do business is close to reaching breaking
point. I really believe that if companies were able to concentrate
on their business rather than making sure that this form and
that form were filled in correctly and by a specific date then more
would survive. This is particularly well represented by the
amount of paper work the average police officer needs to execute
on a daily basis; if this were reduced then would our streets be a
little safer?*

PS, city stockbroker, 34, male,
privately educated

*I have worked in companies of various sizes and the advance of
compliance seems unending. If you log on to an insurance jobsite,*

*compliance and HR vacancies appear to take up 40 per cent.
These people aren't 'producers'. It is a complete waste of time.
I now have made a complete career change, moving from a
Lloyds of London broker that had HR, compliance and spent
most of their time ticking boxes to a reactive drainage and
plumbing company. Half our inbound phone calls are from
companies trying to sell health and safety courses and the like.
You get down a drain surrounded by rats and germs to unblock
a drain that is flooding into a hospice; you haven't time to tick
all the boxes. Again this isn't the Victorian era where health and
safety was not as it is today, but there is risk in life and that means
in the workplace. Of course you cannot have a train driver or
coach driver being on the road for 24 hours without sleep, but
let's get with the real world.*

GH, drainage cleaner, male, 37,
honours degree, privately educated

*Yes. There is far too much paper-filling. A retired teacher spoke
of when she worked in a school for children with special needs
and aimed to give each child the special treatment it needed.
But now you have to ensure that you have covered all that the
regulators think such a child might need, without, of course,
them knowing the specific problems that the child actually has.
The ceramics group had a flood of stories of how filling in
forms and following regulations reduced the chance of being
able to act effectively with the actual situation that they were
having to deal with at work. Time spent on forms reduces time
available for real-life work, in schools, in social work, in running
a small building firm.*

JC, retired religious education teacher,
69, female, public sector

*Yes and yes. The time allocated by senior management to
legislation and regulations has probably increased from about
10 per cent in 1990 to nearer 40 per cent now. If regulation is*

increased much further it will drive businesses to relocate to more benign administrations.

MP, chairman of top FTSE
100 international business, 65, male

When I started the business I was told I needed a fire safety certificate; instinct told me I should put a fire extinguisher in the office. The advice from the local council and fire department was not to. If we placed a fire extinguisher in the office we would need to service it four times per annum and if we didn't we would then be liable. So in summary, better to equip those in the office with nothing rather than an unserviced fire extinguisher – personally, given the option, should fire break out I would rather my employer provided the hope the extinguisher might work rather than leave me with the vain belief that the tap and my coffee cup would be sufficient! I did however complete said fire regulation document and we filed it under 'waste of time' along with our health and safety certificate and the fact we need to get every electrical appliance checked just in case – God forbid – I may one day come to work and find the kettle does not have a safety sticker on it! Policy gone mad… please can we bring back some personal responsibility and the need for good old fashioned common sense – pretty please!

SC, company director, 37, female,
married with two children

Working as an SME means every little thing can stop you doing the day job. In most instances those who are creating a sweeping rule to apply to all are looking at larger, established businesses where people have roles that can burden the extra reporting/ auditing required. When you work within a business where if you run out of paper/toner or need something posted you have to turn everything off, lock up and go to the post office, any amount of additional legislation is a task that will detract from the job of running a business.

SR, single mum/self-employed
business owner, 36, female

Yes more legislation is being introduced all the time, despite all the talk of cutting red tape. The amount of non-productive work to comply with increasing legislation is likewise growing all the time. So much of our GDP is totally taken up with non-productive requirements. Just consider the limited field of letting residential property. Since starting to let property 20 years ago more and more legislation has been introduced which has doubtful benefit and wastes considerable man hours. Examples are:

- *All gas appliances have to be inspected every year. I have now spent more on annual inspections for a gas-fired boiler than the total central heating system cost in the first place. The amount of time in arranging, attending and distributing paperwork is probably not far short of the time taken to install the system.*

- *Energy Performance Certificates have to be obtained before letting a property. A lot of paperwork hardly anybody looks at. I have three EPCs where the estimated energy costs will increase (according to their figures) once the recommended insulation upgrades have been made. Even an old granny would say 'what a load of rubbish'.*

- *Not long ago, as a competent engineer, I could carry out all the electrical and gas work in my properties. Now I can't legally carry out any gas work and only certain electrical work, which has to be done by registered contractors and much associated red tape.*

- *The retention of deposits is now the subject of much regulation.*

- *Twenty years ago letting agreements produced by agencies were typically three pages, now they are considerably longer with the result that most tenants don't read them.*

JP, retired civil servant, 69, male, first class
honours degree in engineering

I believe that businesses in general are becoming more risk-averse and there does seem to be a swing in influence in many businesses (including my own) where the legal departments hold more sway in the day-to-day running of that business. Obviously there need to be boundaries and laws must absolutely be followed but I think this change stifles creativity, which in turn, stifles new lines of income.

CK, sales manager (corporate firm), 45, male,
state education (left school at 16)

9   **Is company growth important? If you have a profitable business does it need to grow?**

It is important for the country but not necessarily for the company. Insisting on growth can lead to risks being taken which may not be the right course of action. A business need only grow to limit the effect of inflation and the increasing costs of regulation. However, if competitors are growing then they may enjoy greater efficiencies which may need to be matched. On balance it is probably wise for companies to try to grow.

MP, chairman of top FTSE
100 international business, 65, male

NO. All the people in the ceramics group said company growth is not necessary – if you are working successfully and can be satisfied with your work and earn enough to live on and to pay employees to live on, then you are successful and growth is irrelevant. Growth is not real if it is based on borrowing. Only hard work, fairly earned, can ever produce real growth.

JC, retired religious education teacher,
69, female, public sector

Economists can and do argue that growth is not essential. This is a bit too complex for me and I'm sure for most people. I think that the two go hand-in-hand, but growth can be dangerous,

*you can overstretch the business, be tempted to plough the profit
to support the growth secured by new, sometimes unknown,
accounts and partnerships and then suddenly find growth stalling
and no cash reserves to fall back on to support new staff and new
machinery and equipment. Our company has grown 22 per cent in
the last financial year and in the present economic conditions this
is a source of pride and encourages employees and directors alike
to work even harder. If we can do that in 2010/2011 what can we
do if good times do return? In an ideal world, I'd take both, but
growth over profit; I think that this increases the potential value
of the company to interested parties.*

GH, drainage cleaner, male,
37, honours degree, privately educated

*For me personally, the purpose of being in business is to achieve
growth consistently. However, growth is not essential if you are
able to achieve a critical mass and sustain it if you have different
ambitions as a business owner. For some business owners,
their aspirations can be achieved with a business offering
a comfortable profit each year.*

SR, single mum/self-employed business
owner, 36, female

*I am going to go against trend here and say no – if you are
making money, happy with your long-term vision, then you don't
need to push yourself to grow. Not every business can grow and
those that do often end up putting others out of business by taking
their market share. We are an island, as a result of that fact we
only have a specific number of customers. We cannot manufacture
people or money – we can sell internationally to grow our market
and our share of the global economy, but ultimately growth
cannot, surely, be achieved year on year. Eventually we will all
have everything we could ever want...*

SC, company director, 37, female,
married with two children

*I think it's all dependent on circumstances, specifically who
runs the business. I come across many SMEs working at capacity
with no appetite to grow further because they believe they will
lose sight of why they started a business in the first place, which
is quite often to be their own boss. These companies still maintain
a healthy balance book and often the service given to their
customers is second to none. By chasing an ever bigger company,
more often than not compromises will have to be made in certain
areas, to the detriment of the original dream or the service
presently offered.*

CK, sales manager (corporate firm),
45, male, state education (left school at 16)

*A new company obviously needs to grow and with that add value
to the wider economy. I think the downfall of some companies is
that they either grow too aggressively or try to push their growth
too far! I think that if a company is profitable and is not under
significant pressure of losing ground to its rivals then it should
take stock and build funds in preparation for either a lean period
or a period during which it can invest and move to the next level
with limited risk.*

PS, city stockbroker, 34, male,
privately educated

*I think far too much emphasis is placed on growth. If a company is
making a good profit and paying fair wages why not be content with
the status quo? Many otherwise viable and successful businesses
have failed by being greedy and trying to grow too quickly. I believe
the health of a nation is better if instead of one large company there
are a number of small to medium-sized companies.*

JP, retired civil servant, 69, male,
first class honours degree in engineering

10 Should businesses have total freedom of speech or should they be
politically correct?

I don't believe that a company should aim to be politically correct, but it must be respectful.

HS, British diplomatic community member,
45, male, lives in Belgium

Total freedom, but even so, use their brains and use tact and common sense. Offend someone these days and the hassle is simply too much of a pain in the backside. To be honest, reactive drainage work doesn't have too many tree-hugging, bearded class warriors working in it; more Sun-reading, hang 'em, flog 'em, deport 'em types.

GH, drainage cleaner, male,
37, honours degree, privately educated

This all depends on what sort of business it is; I think that large companies that put their name to products and events via sponsorship have a duty to be seen to be 'politically correct'. That said there are too many versions of political correctness in this country and I am a firm believer that you can't please everyone all the time!! Smaller firms, more than a responsibility to political correctness, have a responsibility to their communities and general areas. If you have a successful business in the community then why should they not give a little back by any way possible?

PS, city stockbroker, 34, male,
privately educated

I believe everybody should have the freedom to say exactly what they like, without fear of being labelled as different. In a civilized society, we should all be able to express our views, without resorting to insulting behaviour or unkind comments. I believe that by being politically correct, people skirt around issues which can be left to fester, creating a much bigger problem further down the line.

CK, sales manager (corporate firm),
45, male, state education (left school at 16)

Providing businesses don't incite violence or make incorrect claims that could endanger health, then they should be free to say what they like. Political correctness is a relatively recent nonsense that we would be better served if it wasn't tolerated.

JP, retired civil servant, 69, male,
first class honours degree in engineering

Tough question to answer. Businesses should never try to offend deliberately or try to discriminate on purpose, but they should be allowed to express their core values. If you take religion for an example, it would be perfectly reasonable to conceive that a Catholic church would not allow the Mormons to carry out their weekly meeting mid Sunday service, but if a group of Mormons should arrive in tents to make a political point, the businesses they target are pushed to answer the calling and give freedom of speech to all involved. Should business always be so understanding or should the hard nose of corporate ruthlessness come into its own, even if it means handing out tough messages? In a world of social media and TV on mobile phones, when every individual on the street is a potential film crew waiting to capture the moment I think the might of many businesses is paralyzed with fear of doing wrong. Yet to totally eclipse that, we have newspapers carrying out phone hacking to break the boundaries of reporting. Maybe no one really has free speech; we just all voice our opinions in safe environments when we know reprisal is limited.

SC, company director, 37, female,
married with two children

Do businesses have a voice or is it the individuals within the company that are speaking? For me I think a business should not be used to voice the ideals of those sitting behind them. If the chairperson of a large corporation with 4,000 employees makes a public comment that is deemed politically incorrect it should be recognized that he is speaking as an individual and not reflecting the views of every company employee. The business should not

*have an opinion (it is a business and not human with emotions) and
therefore no 'freedom of speech' as it is, as I am sure these questions
are demonstrating, impossible to reflect the views of everyone.*

SR, single mum/self-employed
business owner, 36, female

*My own view is that businesses should be politically correct
but individuals can make a choice about how they speak in their
private lives. The reason a business must be politically correct
is that PC ensures everyone is on a fair playing field and so a
chauvinist/racist/ fanatic-fundamentalist cannot make
employment conditions unfair for fellow employees.*

JC, retired religious education teacher,
69, female, public sector

*Businesses should have as much or as little freedom of speech
as they consider appropriate to the environment in which they
operate. This is a matter of judgement for them and should not be
the subject of any limitation or political correctness.*

MP, chairman of top FTSE 100
international business, 65, male

The world we live in

1   Do we need to worry about health and safety in the workplace as
    much as we do? When is it important?

*Whilst H&S is extremely important, there are clear signs of
administration gone mad. Vast amounts of resources are wasted
with projects like signs above hot taps saying 'Caution, water may
be hot'. H&S imagines scenarios from the sublime to the ridiculous
and will then police this. That said, H&S plays a valuable role in
the workplace as far as personal safety is concerned.*

HS, British diplomatic community member,
45, male, lives in Belgium

*No, there are too many cases when it has resulted in nonsense
and been very counter-productive. While some health and safety is
desirable and some lives have been saved it has been blown out of
all importance and perhaps some of the effort, for example, could
have been diverted to making our roads safer, where deaths and
injuries are considerably greater.*

JP, retired civil servant, 69, male,
first class honours degree in engineering

*This subject is crippling businesses all over the country in
workplaces that it just isn't necessary in and is also linked to
the litigious society that we have created. We have got to a point
that if you trip over at work it is someone else's fault and not
yours for being clumsy. This whole issue comes down to a lack
of responsibility of the individual, as a society we are far too
quick and comfortable to point the finger instead of looking
at our own actions! Where health and safety is paramount is
obvious, places like factories – anywhere that you could genuinely
get injured – need to have strict procedures in place to protect
their employees as far as possible. Again as a country we need
to promote the ability for companies to thrive and the constant
threat of legal action where a company should never be liable is
strangling that ability!*

PS, city stockbroker, 34, male,
privately educated

*Health and safety has a really important part to play. A very good
friend of mine was in a building site when scaffolding collapsed on
him due to a poor installation that was done in a hurry without
any regard for the safety of those on it or under it – that is just
not acceptable and should never happen. Pride should be taken
in people's roles, and their jobs – we should all want to do a good
job to get pride from a job well done and also to make it pleasant
or easier for those that follow behind. Sadly I think society no
longer does much for pride, cynical though that may be – I feel*

we all 'do what we are paid for'. Only a few people go the extra mile to help those despite the act gaining nothing for them. But even sadder is the next step – when people look for fault in what others do to try to 'sue' them or take them to court for failing to carry out the correct job. Health and safety should exist to protect people from negligence – only ever in my opinion in the workplace and never to the extremes we have allowed it to seep into our lives. All health and safety should be run in conjunction with common sense! If the floor is wet, walk carefully; if someone has cleaned their drive of snow yet the ice has frosted it up again, tread carefully. If you break into someone's house and hurt yourself then you should NOT be allowed to take them to court as the 'staircase did not meet the building regulations' and you fell! We have become a victim society. We should protect our innocent, the working people and the public but only in line with common sense and the law. In my mind you cannot and should not be protected by the law when you are breaking it. If you break the law you are not protected by it.

SC, company director, 37, female,
married with two children

We absolutely need to worry about H&S in the workplace. The safety of employees must be top of the list for all companies. However, a cottage industry has sprung up in H&S with some over-the-top requirements (hard hats in road construction?). A common sense approach would benefit both employees and employers and hush the 'its political correctness gone mad' brigade.

CK, sales manager (corporate firm), 45, male,
state education (left school at 16)

It depends on what industry we work in. Health and safety has gone too far. We have recently taken on a contract where the health and safety section in the job worksheets is greater in space than the area to describe works that may have been complex and taken 12 hours to complete, whereas the H&S risks may have been minimal. The number of H&S consultancy companies and bodies that companies need to register with are everywhere. We take call after call from such companies and organizations trying to peddle their wares. This turns you off H&S. However, H&S in a Dungeness Reactor B is a tad more important than at an office in Bishops Square. And, lest we forget such tragedies as the King's Cross tube fire, Bradford City FC, Piper Alpha, MRSA outbreaks and many more, health and safety is essential, but must be realistic, designed by professionals rather than graduate desk dwellers that have never done the work that they have now come so much to hinder.

GH, drainage cleaner, male,
37, honours degree, privately educated

Health and safety needs to be seriously reconsidered, as it is to the extreme and is nonsensical in most instances when I consider my personal working situation. I don't understand why rules are created that are so demanding on the employer with no responsibility on the individual. Are we really at the point of not being able to ever step over a wire for fear of tripping and having an accident that could result in a legal claim? We have watched other countries go through the culture of 'blame' and thousands of lawsuits over trivial matters and we have simply jumped on the bandwagon. We shouldn't have to worry about health and safety as much as we do but we have to! That said, there are obviously working environments where health and safety is paramount, and the rules are there to safeguard employees. We could use the thought processes of a teenager to work out when health and safety guidelines should be implemented.

SR, single mum/self-employed
business owner, 36, female

Moderation is needed in every interpretation of the law. Some little 'dictators' like to follow the legislation with an over-detailed exactitude and miss the basic point of the law.

*On the other hand carelessness that can lead to dangerous
situations and even accidents shows that legislation is needed.*

JC, retired religious education teacher,
69, female, public sector

*Health and safety is an important contributor to the workplace
environment and many good practices have emerged as a result.
However, some people in the Health and Safety Executive are
either ill-trained or stupid and some of their pronouncements are
seriously to the detriment of society in general. In particular, the
effect that over-zealousness has on the development of children
is to be strongly condemned. Life is a risk and the risks and
rewards are presently out of balance and, if the trend continues,
will eventually render the population as feeble, cosseted and
unproductive. This is an important issue that MUST be tackled.*

MP, chairman of top FTSE
100 international business, 65, male

2 **Does the current benefit system work; does it help those who need
it or reward laziness?**

*It helps some who are deserving but also rewards a lot who
are undeserving. A separate e-mail I received demonstrates the
stupidity of the present situation as regards pensions.*

E-mail that was circulated recently by an anonymous source:

Dear Prime Minister The RT. Hon. David Cameron, MP. I wish to ask
you a Question: - 'Is This True?'. I refer to the Pension Reality Check.
Are you aware of the following?

The British Government provides the following financial assistance:-

BRITISH OLD AGED PENSIONER
(bearing in mind they worked hard and paid their Income Tax and
National Insurance contributions to the British Government all their
working life)
Weekly allowance: £106.00?

ILLEGAL IMMIGRANTS/REFUGEES LIVING IN BRITAIN
(No Income Tax and National Insurance contribution whatsoever)
Weekly allowance: £250.00

BRITISH OLD AGED PENSIONER
Weekly Spouse Allowance: £25.00?

ILLEGAL IMMIGRANTS/REFUGEES LIVING IN BRITAIN
Weekly Spouse Allowance: £225.00

BRITISH OLD AGED PENSIONER
Additional Weekly Hardship Allowance: £0.00?

ILLEGAL IMMIGRANTS/REFUGEES LIVING IN BRITAIN
Additional Weekly Hardship Allowance: £100.00
A British old age pensioner is no less hard up than an illegal
immigrant/refugee yet receives nothing

BRITISH OLD AGED PENSIONER

TOTAL YEARLY BENEFIT £6,000?

ILLEGAL IMMIGRANTS/REFUGEES LIVING IN BRITAIN

TOTAL YEARLY BENEFIT: £29,900
Please read all and then forward to all your contacts so that we can
lobby for a decent state pension.
After all, the average pensioner has paid taxes and contributed to the
growth of this country for the last 40 to 60 years.

*The above e-mail highlights the ridiculous situation, and this also
exists in other forms of welfare. Self-inflicted injuries such as having
more children should not allow people to claim higher benefits. It
is a sad reflection of the present state of affairs that people can be
better off claiming benefits than going out to work.*

MP, chairman of top FTSE
100 international business, 65, male

The benefit system is seriously flawed and has numerous problems but the biggest problem is finding a solution where you help just those that need it, support those that would rather not rely on benefits and avoid those 'working the system'. Take a situation, female in her mid-30s, married and working part-time around the children who are at school. Has a limited income due to the part-time nature of her work. When her personal circumstances change as she separates from her husband and loses his income into the house, the benefit system assists in paying credits to ensure she is able to provide for the family. However, she meets someone new who has no parental responsibility towards her children but they would like to live together. Suddenly any assistance is removed from the financial equation but the responsibility falls to the individual who earns more but has no responsibility towards the children. Does that work in providing stability and security for the children? There are many, many people who are not incentivized to work as they are able to live a reasonable life without the need to earn a higher income (if any) and there are those who cannot afford to leave the system even when they want to. Do we reward laziness in some instances? Yes, but the system works for the majority when they are in need. Better transition phases are needed to incentivize over a period of time or bonuses paid for working rather than long-term benefits paid to those who are not.

SR, single mum/self-employed business
owner, 36, female

No – in short I think the current system will never work as it comes with too much legacy – the foundations with which it is built are shaky and the structure resting on those shaky foundations is full of holes, loopholes, legacy issues and Elastoplast holding together a decaying structure. We need to wipe the slate clean and start again, helping those that need benefits and not those that 'live off the state'. We should never be in a situation that means that a system is put together, not means-tested or

*benchmarked because the cost of checking if the system is fair
would be more than just blanket-paying everybody – whether they
deserve it or not. A ludicrous situation. How can running a few
analysis models to check that if you remove the family allowance
at the 40 per cent tax rate mean that you will penalize some of the
families who work so hard to keep their heads above water? How?
If that is true and we cannot assess what is fair and what is correct
without so much investment in government that it makes the
process flawed, then we must have got something wrong with the
benefits system. We must surely be able to make it simpler, fairer
and cheaper to run. Let's give the money to those that need it – not
the one-size-fits-all for process purposes.*

SC, company director, 37, female,
married with two children

*We discussed this and felt that the current benefit system does
not encourage people to work, on the other hand when there is
so little chance of employment around we do need benefits that
enable the unemployed to live with some dignity. This of course
will not encourage the work-shy to get work. The trouble is
basically that people are so varied in ability that there is no
easy way to be fair.*

JC, retired religious education teacher,
69, female, public sector

*The benefit system in our country is not good enough; we don't
regulate those that claim well enough. There are far too many
people on benefit that have no right to it at all; we reward laziness
by handing out money for injuries that don't exist and houses
to those that play the game! The UK should have one neutral
medical centre that anyone wanting to be signed off as unable
to work would go to. This system would drastically reduce the
number of people on incapacity benefit and save the government
huge sums of money. The whole system needs an overhaul so that
the state can manage effectively those that claim... benefits are an*

important aspect of society, however I feel that some in society see it as a free ride and that is not fair on those that work hard and pay their taxes!

PS, city stockbroker,
34, male, privately educated

The current benefit system doesn't work and can't be afforded any longer. There are of course some who genuinely need help but there is far too much abuse and in many cases it encourages people to do nothing to help themselves. I believe nobody should be paid to do nothing and should for example have to undergo full-time training to get unemployment benefit. When the welfare state was first introduced it was never intended for people to do nothing to improve their chances of work. William Beveridge, one of the founders of the welfare state explicitly said that the dole should be conditional upon attendance at a work or training centre. To keep the cost low those unemployed with skills can do the training. This will improve the nation's skill base and make being employed more attractive to the work-shy. It is surely economic suicide to allow foreigners into the country to do the jobs that could be done by unemployed people we are paying not to work. I know of cases where men with degrees have calculated the optimum number of children so that all benefits will be sufficient to avoid having to work. Too many young girls have seen having a baby as the way to their own home and a life dependent on the state.
Too many people look on benefits as a right, whereas the ethos needs to change so that people believe they must still make contributions to society to get help. The generous and easily obtained benefits have produced an underclass of people who some have argued are turning back the process of evolution.

JP, retired civil servant, 69, male,
first class honours degree in engineering

This all depends on your view of working. If by working, you mean that disabled people and people who have hit rock bottom receive an allowance to live on, yes it's working. If on the other hand, you mean that the system is open to abuse and people hide behind it, then no, it's not fit for purpose. I feel proud to live in a society whereby we look after those who most need help and by and large, I feel we do this very well. However, the system has always been open to abuse for as long as I remember and it continues to be so. I'm sure we all have stories and examples of this but as long ago as the late 80s, I was aware of a girl whose parents took her to court to evict her, solely so she could climb to the top of the housing ladder with her baby. I feel we should be much stricter in enforcing these rules but we also need to instil a sense of pride in people, so they fight for the right to earn a living and to get themselves off of benefits.

CK, sales manager (corporate firm),
45, male, state education (left school at 16)

Rather like asking whether or not injecting heroin is good for your health. No. We spend more on the welfare state than education, defence, transport and policing put together. Like HMRC, it is a shambles. I've signed on, the system is pathetic. Work for 45 years, never miss a day, lose your job, get £65 a week in JSA but as someone who is 'contribution' assessed, from that £65 you still have to pay for any prescriptions at £7.40 or a filling at the dentist at £48. A homeowner with a mortgage with no payment protection, you get no help. On the other hand, pay rent and they pay your 'housing benefit'. Aged 18 and a single mother, council house and the same £65 in JSA but 'income' assessed (meaning you've never paid into the system) and prescriptions and dental treatment all free. Why do young men from Africa and Kosovo not stay in Calais but risk everything by trying to hitch under lorries to the UK? And housing benefit? Just incredulous. For this once great nation, hope has almost been extinguished.

GH, drainage cleaner, male,
37, honours degree, privately educated

3 Why do governments want or need country growth and is this
   sustainable long-term?

*Growth is needed to expand the economy so that more taxes
can be raised and the wealth and infrastructure improved.
This is a commendable target. Internationally, growth can only
be sustained long-term if the world population is expanding.
This is not good as the world is already over-populated.
Growth can however be achieved by an increase in productivity
which would allow the population to remain static.*

MP, chairman of top FTSE
100 international business, 65, male

*I believe that growth within a country is important; however
growth should not be forced by increasing a country's debt
position. If a country grows organically then that can only be a
good thing; however if that growth comes with the use of debt
and leverage then this can (as we are seeing in Europe currently)
prove fatal. We must all learn to control our greed and regain the
ability to be patient!*

PS, city stockbroker,
34, male, privately educated

*This is one for Balls, Osborne, Merv the Swerve and
disciples of Adam Smith and J. M. Keynes. I'd be more
concerned that the chaps who now make economic policy
have no experience of real working life and the leaders of
all three main political parties have followed exactly the same
path. PPE, political researcher, MP, junior minister/shadow
minister, leader/PM. I draw you to the broad ranging work
and business experience and career of the man who presided
over the biggest boom and bust this country has ever seen.
'From 1976 to 1980 Gordon Brown was employed as a lecturer
in politics at Glasgow College of Technology. From 1980 he
worked as a journalist at Scottish Television. He also worked as*

a tutor for the Open University'. Not really any different from asking a chap who has been a milkman to pilot a space shuttle without an ounce of training, but the brilliantly educated masses elected him and Tony and must, therefore, reap the wind that they sowed.

GH, drainage cleaner, male,
37, honours degree, privately educated

I believe every government would like to see growth for one very simple reason, votes. Growth means more revenue for the treasury and more revenue in turn translates to vote-winning initiatives for improving voters' lives. Now, this in itself is not a bad thing, I believe those that seek election should want to improve the lives of their citizens, along with protecting the country (be that economically or in a real sense). Growth means not having to tax citizens too hard, something I've no quibble with. Growth can be sustainable long-term but this would need to have solid foundations. In the UK, the financial sector is not what you build a long-term sustainable economic growth policy on.

CK, sales manager (corporate firm),
45, male, state education (left school at 16)

A country does not need to grow any more than a company does. All that a government should do is seek to rule a country that grows enough food for its people, or produces enough to sell in exchange for food, so that no one need starve. Also people need to be paid enough to be able to develop new inventions. Money should be for useful activities, not for mere aggrandizement, big cars, posh frocks.

JC, retired religious education teacher,
69, female, public sector

Government want growth so that more taxes are raised and therefore more money can be borrowed and they can 'bribe' the voters with short-term tax cuts. There is an old saying that only politicians, economists and fools believe you can have growth year on year. Taking this to an extreme, we will either have so many people we can't move or we will spend all our time making or buying things, or even worse complying with yet more red tape. Governments and some economists seem to think that the overriding measure of a country's economic performance is the GDP. Labour were particularly guilty of this and were content to allow extensive immigration to increase the GDP; what they didn't seem capable of understanding is that if the population increases by 10 per cent but GDP only increases by 6 per cent, then we are in recession despite apparent growth. The greatest mistake our politicians have made is to allow so much immigration. Whilst we have benefited from some very able and decent immigrants we have also let in considerably more very undesirable people. The whole makeup of the country has radically changed and this has happened because people are too scared to oppose immigration in case they are considered racist. Throughout history and all over the world different ethnicities have proved to be unable to live in harmony with each other, and I think the recent demographic change in the UK is an absolute disaster which will only become more apparent as time goes by. Apart from which the increase in population is something this small country cannot accommodate.

JP, retired civil servant, 69, male,
first class honours degree in engineering

I run a small SME – I cannot grow any more quickly than I am and soon we will have reached capacity. Should we invest more to stretch ourselves when we are profitable, should we push ourselves to the limits at a time when the country is either in recession or fighting to stay out of it one month to the next? I am sure for some economic reason everything must always grow, but in my simple mind this cannot be possible. I know without growth the taxes taken by the government don't increase or the rate of business tax does not grow to help pay for expanding costs, but there must be a limit to growth – eventually we must all be the right size? The need for constant expansion is only driven by higher costs to support the economy but if everything stopped then so must the need to support the increase. The financial bank bubble that burst was built of sub-prime lending but in simplistic terms that must just be individuals being lent too much money, without the means to re-pay it and without the ability to grow their income to substantiate it. Growth can ruin lives, push people and businesses to the limit – in a throwaway society should we not be happy with what we have got? Growth in the right areas is essential, but we can't force it. To get growth without enough water to feed it, then it will shrivel and die; would it be better never to plant the seed?

SC, company director,
37, female, married with two children

Our country needs to grow as we are expanding in our numbers, those who are elderly and need to be provided for and those who need to be educated in their youth. Growth is also about puffing up your chest against other countries that would like to take control of our industries. We have to show that we are strong as a nation. Britain does have the additional problem of our age as a nation and our size. To continue to increase our population in a country that has many towns and cities requiring investment to update their aging facilities and building or start building on new land to provide adequate housing requires massive investment from the government. Our government is only able to invest if we grow as a country. Is this sustainable long-term? I think our regular periods of recession are an indication that this is not sustainable long-term and we have to slow the growth for periods of time where we concentrate on stabilizing the economy before growth can start again.

SR, single mum/self-employed
business owner, 36, female

*With an aging population, it is important that the country
maintains growth and revenue to satisfy the demands put on the
infrastructure. With growth there is a continuing revenue source
for the public coffers through taxes either direct or indirect.
This is sustainable as long as the country remains competitive
and social mobility and adaptation to changes is possible.*

HS, British diplomatic community member,

45, male, lives in Belgium

4 **How can the UK be more competitive in manufacturing; is this
important?**

*The UK can be more competitive by either reducing input
costs eg labour; increasing productivity or investing in more
efficient equipment. Removing layers of regulation would also
help. Yes, for the UK to survive in the present difficult world
environment, it is important that continued increases
in competiveness are achieved.*

MP, chairman of top FTSE

100 international business, 65, male

*Tricky. Where does one start? Personally I blame the Nazis.
They started the war. They then overran France. The Americans
were late. The tide of the war turned. Germany and Japan were
pummelled into total destruction by air and land. War ends,
USA pulls the economic rug from under Britain. She knows we
will never turn communist. She ploughs billions into Germany
and Japan to avert this communist threat. France, her major
cities never flattened, has much of her industry intact. The USA
was never bombed. Germany and Japan start almost from
scratch. Britain is in between, a victor, but with heavily damaged
but not destroyed industrial infrastructure. In 1945 we built 59
per cent of the world's ships, more cars than even America in
1950. Take the shipyards. I believe there were 30 on the Clyde
alone. You are a shipyard owner, you have a full order book for*

three years. Are you going to shut down and totally modernize
whilst orders are aplenty? No chance. The unions, the shipyard
machinery, one machine operated by eight men, are you going to
support modernization that results in a machine operated by two
men instead of eight? No. Then suddenly it is 1960 and the new
shipyards of the countries that had been reduced to total rubble
and then been plied with billions to avert the communist threat
start building ships in half the time and at half the cost. You have
a cargo company in Australia, and oil company in Spain, where
are you going to place your order, the Clyde or the Elbe, Wearside
or Tokyo? 2012 four new Royal Navy tankers, ordered with
Daewoo. Enough said. However much we want to turn the clock
back to the halcyon days of being the workshop of the world we
can't. Educational standards are poor, the infrastructure and skills
gone. It is sad, but I cannot see how it was going to evolve in any
other way. So where are we left? Lighter, higher-tech industries,
but again, with poor education, how can we compete with China,
Japan and the USA? Just think of the creators, the inventors, the
industrialists, the engineers and the like who adorn our banknotes
and our street signs: Watt, Brunel, Cockerell, Barnes Wallis,
Whittle, Rolls and Royce, Stephenson, one could go on and on.
In 50 years Britain will still be using the same people on her bank
notes because where are their successors? Dyson and... er...?

GH, drainage cleaner, male,
37, honours degree, privately educated

Sometimes as a nation we have to work with what we do best.
While we have many talented individuals around the country
who are more than able to produce and manufacture amazing
products, look at who we are competing against. Countries that
have made manufacturing their main industry are so far ahead
of the game against us. It would be great to be able to buy
British-made products but when cost is such a major decision-
maker when purchasing anything at all, we do not have the
infrastructure to produce on the scale of competitive countries.

*It is more important that we understand our strengths as a
country and maximize our opportunities.*

SR, single mum/self-employed
business owner, 36, female

*From my point of view, I believe when we talk about
manufacturing in the UK, we need to change the perception
about making physical things. Going forward, our manufacturing
will be in the design and creation of such things as hardware
and software in the IT sector. No pun intended but the boat has
sailed for this nation being a manufacturing giant and this role
will now be fulfilled by countries in the Far East (in the main).
Being an island nation with limited natural resources, we need
to import most of the raw materials used and right from the off,
we're adding costs to our manufacturing process. Allied to this is
the cost of living in the UK and wages that needed to be paid to
support workers and I no longer think we can compete globally
anymore in the manufacture of physical goods.*

CK, sales manager (corporate firm),
45, male, state education (left school at 16)

*Our government must help UK firms more. We must turn more
of a blind eye to EU requirements as other countries do.
Government should have helped our shipbuilders, our steel
makers, our car manufacturers, our nuclear industry etc, to keep
them as thriving industries with British owners. We should not
be using taxpayers' money to buy foreign goods when British
companies could be used.*

JP, retired civil servant, 69, male,
first class honours degree in engineering

*As the UK cannot feed itself it does need to manufacture things
and ideas that other countries want to purchase or to do swaps –
food for goods. But morality has to play a part, we should never
seek to use the labour of poor people in poor countries in order to*

sell their goods at bargain prices. Money should never be the chief aim of commerce; commerce is only valuable in so far as it works for the good of all.

JC, retired religious education teacher,
69, female, public sector

As part of an old western developed economy, it is hard for manufacturing in the UK to remain competitive in old economy areas like steel production. However, the UK remains competitive in the assembly of cars for example. There is however a problem in this sector due to the uncompetitive social laws found in other European countries. The fact the UK is able to offer cheap production lines works so long as the economy is experiencing good growth. However, in times of economic gloom, it is much easier to close down a UK manufacturing/assembly facility than one in continental Europe due to the worker protection found there. It is also naïve to think that Europe will do anything to counter this due to local politics at play.

HS, British diplomatic community member,
45, male, lives in Belgium

This in my view is the single most important part of our ability to grow out of the financial crisis and avert the chance of another serious recession. The UK must get back what the Labour party managed to let slip and allow the manufacturing sector to thrive once more. As a nation we have always been at the forefront of invention and manufacturing and it is criminal that we no longer hold that status. We must focus on the needs of the nations that are recovering more quickly than ourselves and create a manufacturing sector that takes advantage of those nations' growth. In my opinion emerging markets like Brazil, India and established markets like the USA will be the key to our ability to rekindle our greatest skill... invention.

PS, city stockbroker, 34, male, privately educated

*The UK needs to make something – the square mile in the city
full of bankers and brokers are a lifeline of income. We need
to be able to be a nation of great output too. We used to have
so much to be proud of: the stamp 'Made in Great Britain'
was something to be worn with pride, it stood for quality, for
exceptional standard, for amazing individuality. In a world where
global warming is increasing and where we push every part of a
business to be eco-friendly and aware of its green footprint, we
import everything. Seasonal vegetables are no more; we can have
strawberries all year round with a huge carbon footprint attached.
Now I am a sceptic when it comes to global warming, the fact
that Formula One exists burning fuel for fun, I see no reason my
car tax should increase to cover my carbon output! When China
creates a new coal-fired power station practically every other week
I am confused – I cannot buy my preferred light bulbs anymore.
Digital waste is terrible – the dumping of said manufacturing
parts is polluting huge areas of poorer counties. We need to get
back to our roots and start producing things we can all be proud
of as a nation.*

SC, company director, 37, female,
married with two children

5　**Have business ethics deteriorated in the last 12 years since the turn
of the last century?**

*Ethics across the board have deteriorated in the last 12 years,
continuing the trend of the previous 20 years. Some of the tax
dodges employed by large companies are totally immoral. There is an
increasing trend to expect some employees to give much more than a
fair day's work while directors often do little and award themselves
huge pay rewards. The extent of loyalty to employees and the country
appears to be far less these days. Take the case of Dyson who had a
successful business in this country, but in my view became greedy and
decided to manufacture abroad to save on labour costs. It may be
considered sound commercial sense but it let down its UK workforce*

and undermined its contribution to the UK economy. Perhaps we should impose heavy import duties on such employers.

JP, retired civil servant, 69, male,
first class honours degree in engineering

Impossible to answer. What businesses, what sectors, any particular companies in mind? If they have deteriorated, it only mirrors the nation's moral decline since the 1960s.

GH, drainage cleaner, male,
37, honours degree, privately educated

No. It's just that now, any ethical question enters the public domain faster due to better communication.

HS, British diplomatic community member,
45, male, lives in Belgium

The ceramic group thought the answer was No. BUT there has been change in some values; there has been a growth in venal ambitions and a loss of the feeling that it is as important to consider the good of others as of oneself. Everyone needs to recognize that a family, a community, a nation should be taken care of as much as the care given to the individual.

JC, retired religious education teacher,
69, female, public sector

Personally I don't think so and for one main reason, accountability. Historically big business has been run by a clique of powerful figures and as such has been unapproachable/ unaccountable. Nowadays, and especially since the banking crisis, shareholders, the media and the general public are less likely or prepared to put up with secrecy. There is barely a week goes by without a shareholder revolt against an industry giant being discussed, whether it's about money or ethics, so this has got to be a good sign going forward. The next step in business ethics will be around corporate social responsibility and companies'

*environmental records. At the moment this is stage managed or
'green-washed' if you prefer, by PR managers but as with the
examples mentioned earlier, interested parties will not put up
with this for much longer.*

CK, sales manager (corporate firm),
45, male, state education (left school at 16)

*Yes, the notion of greed has taken over in most boardrooms!
We are no longer happy as businesses to compete with each
other – the driver for business is now to be the biggest and the
best and damn the consequences. You only have to look at RBS
for a perfect example. RBS began to swallow smaller financial
entities in order to gain easy footholds in markets in which it
wasn't currently active and also in order to take out potential
competition. It became too large and even as the world told it
not to, the board went ahead with one of the most ill-conceived
takeovers in history... every empire falls eventually! Individuals
across every sector are happy to step on the next guy to get to
the next level. I am all for competitiveness; however, underhand
tactics and ripping off customers and clients should not be part
of the 'game'!*

PS, city stockbroker,
34, male, privately educated

*Business has become harsher but ethics have got better as we
have so many pieces of legislation telling us we have to be ethical
and politically correct within our businesses. How could it have
deteriorated when the government has such rigid guidelines in
how we should behave? We have to be prepared to give reasons
to every person who doesn't get offered employment, we have to
ensure we are fair in our handling of every situation and we have
to be equal to all employees at all times.*

SR, single mum/self-employed
business owner, 36, female

*In many cases, business ethics have improved over the last
12 years. The increase in media investigations is probably a good
thing but does give the impression that ethics have deteriorated
when in fact the vast majority of businesses are more ethical.*

MP, chairman of top FTSE
100 international business, 65, male

6   If bankers are the devil, then what are tobacco companies?

*You could say, if bankers are the devil then the tobacco companies
are even worse. However, we all have the option not to smoke
but we don't really have the option not to use banks whose
exploitation of this makes them perhaps the greater evil. There is
the argument that smokers help the economy with the huge tax
receipts and by dying younger also save on pension costs.*

JP, retired civil servant, 69, male,
first class honours degree in engineering

*If tobacco companies are deemed to be worse than the devil,
then the government should have the courage to legislate against
them. But to be consistent, they would also have to legislate
against other businesses that benefit from addiction eg gambling,
alcohol etc. An unlikely scenario due to the taxes raised and the
employment opportunities.*

MP, chairman of top FTSE
100 international business, 65, male

*I believe that as long as they are allowed to then tobacco
companies have the right to produce their products. I do
think that governments across the world should tax cigarettes
to the point that people wouldn't be able to afford to smoke;
that said, the large companies are such important contributors
to the exchequer that it would almost be cutting their nose off
to spite their face! British American Tobacco is currently worth
£62.5 billion and the government would not be in a position to*

bring down the tobacco industry and lose the revenue they create! Tobacco companies create products that have the ability to kill people and the public buy them – who are the fools?

PS, city stockbroker,
34, male, privately educated

We will all die, smoke or not. People have been smoking 'the weed' for hundreds of years. Any fool knows inhaling smoke and chemicals isn't the brightest thing to do, but then a smoker pays lots of tax and odds on won't be around to claim his pension, so actually the tobacco company provides billions in tax (corporation tax and tax on the ciggies themselves) to the exchequer, whilst killing us early. The Lord works in mysterious ways.

GH, drainage cleaner, male,
37, honours degree, privately educated

'In banks we trust.' That is if we know nothing about how banks work. Modern financial trading meant that the banks were looking for massive returns with very little risk. Or so it seemed. Most people's idea of a bank was that they would use our savings to finance mortgages and business loans. This mentality disappeared at the end of the 80s when commercial banks started entering the merchant sector. There was little transparency in the banking sector which is why, when the meltdown occurred, nobody really understood. The banking sector was also living in denial, and this is the only comparison that can be made with the tobacco sector. We now know that tobacco kills and are able to make a choice as to whether we smoke or not. Banks however...? We can't do without them.

HS, British diplomatic community member,
45, male, lives in Belgium

At first the ceramics group felt that this question did not give sensible comparisons; bankers can be compared to footballers and other organizations that pay some of its top wage earners far too much whereas tobacco companies need to be compared with other sellers of drugs. (The legal status of tobacco is irrelevant here.) However, after further discussion we did agree that there is a genuine comparison between bankers and tobacco companies in that both are legally entitled to do something that is pleasant for a few (pay a lot for shoddy work – banks left people who had trusted the investors without their money) and tobacco companies sold cigarettes (but then left people with ill health and the NHS with problems). Both are bad for the country in general.

JC, retired religious education teacher,
69, female, public sector

I imagine the short answer would be legalized drug pushers (as an ex-smoker, I'm rather pious about this subject; aren't we all?) But if we say that, then I imagine we should also include all vineyards, brewers etc. Both, in the long term (and if abused by the user), will produce catastrophic effects but tobacco is so much more emotive than alcohol. Governments could do so much more to stop us smoking but I personally think they like the revenue this brings in with taxes, so should be as culpable as the tobacco companies themselves.

CK, sales manager (corporate firm),
45, male, state education (left school at 16)

Tobacco companies are essential to our country and are perhaps the devil's rich little brother? Against the odds of being widely known to cause thousands of deaths and diseases, each and every year individuals willingly start smoking. These are companies who are providing a legal product with limited advertising opportunities, risks prominently displayed on packaging and a huge additional cost added on to discourage the products from being attractively sold. They are not even allowed to be on display in supermarkets and are hidden behind screens. The taxes raised just from tobacco sales are considerable and as a country we would struggle if every smoker just gave up tomorrow! How would we cover the shortfall in income from taxes; who would cover the medical cover for those who have already been affected from years of smoking? The tobacco companies could be seen negatively but they are essential to our economy and are honest about the products they sell. May not be ideal but at least the warnings are on the box!

SR, single mum/self-employed
business owner, 36, female

7   Should the UK be allying with the USA or Europe?

'Keep your friends close and your enemies closer' covers this one. Yes, we are not big enough to sit alone on issues and need the comfort of numbers from other larger countries or groups of countries. We are not the only country that looks for allies, every country is doing the same and it is necessary to have others agree with our stance on important issues to give us confidence in our position. We should however be allying on topics individually rather than having to hold hands with another country regardless of whether we agree with them on absolutely everything.

SR, single mum/self-employed
business owner, 36, female

UK shouldn't be allying with either the USA or Europe. We should go our own way, following the path adopted by Norway who is in such a strong financial position. Although much has been said about our special relationship with the US they have not always been a great ally. They did their best to reduce our power and influence after the Second World War and certainly gave us no support in the Falklands war. They dragged us into an ill-conceived war in Iraq when we should really have done something about Iran. Did George Bush know the difference? The only thing to be said for them is that they speak English or something closely resembling it. As for Europe, we could do without all the

*interference in our domestic affairs and the large contributions
we have to make to its cost particularly the huge amounts going to
European farmers. Being in Europe has made it much harder
to restrict immigration.*

JP, retired civil servant,
69, male, first class honours degree in engineering

*Neither. Maybe alignment with India, China or Africa would be a
better idea. The Western world is in decline and fall and we should
make new alliances before others beat us to it.*

MP, chairman of top FTSE
100 international business, 65, male

*We are Europeans. Fact. We are on the same continental shelf. We
are not a sub-piece of America. As a small island we do need allies,
but we need to be as independent as possible. USA is powerful,
but we don't want to be a small flea on its backside. Scotland and
Wales need to co-operate with England. Independence of any one
of the three would be silly. The UK needs to be united. (Northern
Ireland, in the opinion of the ceramic group, would do better to
commit itself to the other part of Ireland.)*

JC, retired religious education teacher,
69, female, public sector

*The US economy is strengthening at a better rate than
Europe's and as such the UK should be trying to take advantage
of this strength. If we create an export culture to the US and the
other dominating global economies then we will be able to drag
ourselves out of the crisis faster. Yes, the initial cost of getting our
manufacturing and engineering sectors in place to maximize their
ability to sell to these economies will hurt; however, we as
a nation will again be able to call ourselves frontrunners once we
re-establish ourselves!*

PS, city stockbroker,
34, male, privately educated

Without wishing to sit on the fence I believe we should not restrict ourselves with just these two. The emerging industrial nations (Brazil, China, India etc) will begin to wield more power as the years pass and not to forge alliances with them would be foolhardy. Ideologically we are more closely aligned to the US but to me we think more about this 'special relationship' than they do, so why would you concentrate all of your efforts here? Europe geographically should be our ally but culturally it is a hotch-potch so we would struggle to completely integrate.

CK, sales manager (corporate firm),
45, male, state education (left school at 16)

Europe. It is through naivety and media headlines that UK citizens think that they would be better aligned to the US. Whilst the US may preach liberalism, it is strictly under its terms and the constant in-battles between the warring parties of congress or the president means that US industry is always favoured. European trade theoretically is done on a level playing field and covered by differing treaties that encourage the internal market. Where I disagree with the European model is on the subject of fiscal union.

HS, British diplomatic community member,
45, male, lives in Belgium

The Yanks were late in the last war. Obama screwed us with that 'British Petroleum' gut-wrenching rhetoric when more Americans were employed by BP than Brits; they pulled the rug from under us in 1945 when they withdrew their nuclear secrets and after we had started their programme for them in 1942 by pooling resources, and shafted us at Suez in 1956. And after all that I'd have them by my side every time. Visit Omaha Beach military cemetery and see the 9,000 graves of young 'farm boys' who never got off the beach and you'll see why. Personally I feel closer to an Australian who couldn't be further away: he drinks tea, has the same Queen and plays cricket; a Frenchman 25 miles across the channel, totally alien. I'm still confident if push came to shove our

cousins across the pond would be with us in our darkest hour,
we have our squabbles, but in the words of George W. Bush 'the
United States of America has no closer friend than Great Britain'.
USA or France/Germany/Spain/Italy, no contest – I'd take the
colonials every time.

GH, drainage cleaner, male,
37, honours degree, privately educated

8   Will the Eurozone remain in two years?

Probably not, but if it is, it will be accompanied by hyper-inflation.
MP, chairman of top FTSE
100 international business, 65, male

Probably, but hopefully not. It was fantasy in the beginning,
and it remains unworkable. If the economy of Newcastle
struggles to merge with the economy of London under the
same tax and fiscal regulation, how were Germany and Greece
ever going to integrate without political and fiscal union?
The one thing we can thank Gordon 'the Clown' Brown for is
keeping us out.

GH, drainage cleaner, male,
37, honours degree, privately educated

Not in its present form. Greece will certainly default on its debts.
We should leave the Eurozone; we are already becoming second-
class members and will shortly have all the disadvantages and no
benefits. The European agricultural policy has been incredibly
expensive and ineffectual; it is outrageous that it is paying millions
of pounds each year to some of our richest people, many of whom
are only making a pretence to farm.

JP, retired civil servant, 69, male,
first class honours degree in engineering

I don't believe so; I think that a single currency across nations
that set their own interest rates and manage their own economies

*is flawed. Being able to devalue its currency is the key to a
country's ability to survive as is being proved by Greece currently.
The different mentalities between European countries mean that a
single currency cannot exist effectively!*

PS, city stockbroker,
34, male, privately educated

*The Eurozone should remain, simply because those involved have
made a commitment for the future of their countries. It is supposed
to be more of a marriage with longevity rather than a boyfriend
who suddenly loses his job and can't buy dinner anymore! In a
stable economy the euro worked, trading in a common currency
and favouring countries on trade deals is an ideal way of working,
keeping everyone's economies strong and assisting each other's
growth. When the economy slowed, the countries should have been
more ready to discuss forecasted problems and seek assistance
immediately to steady any decline and other countries who were
able to should have stepped in. Every country in the Eurozone
joined in the hope of reaping the benefits: with that comes the need
for support in difficult times. Should the Eurozone remain? Yes.
Will the Eurozone remain? Probably not. Once one country pulls
out, it will be a domino effect.*

SR, single mum/self-employed
business owner, 36, female

Yes, but probably not the finance.

JC, retired religious education teacher,
69, female, public sector

*Yes, though perhaps not in its present form. European leaders
have taken a plaster to try and heal a massive flesh wound. The
euro has brought huge benefits to the European market place
which unfortunately the UK hasn't been able to see. One area of
weakness though is the 'one-size-fits-all' mentality which means*

that the currency is unable to react at a local level through national central banks and tends to play to the larger economies.

HS, British Diplomatic Community Member,
45, male, lives in Belgium

I believe it will but only because too many countries have so much invested in it (both literally and ideologically) that they cannot afford it to fail. If the question was will the euro prosper, then I don't believe it will as it is contaminated. It needs and wants more countries to join but this is indeed in itself one of its main weaknesses. Also, as current events have borne out, it is overly reliant on Germany and France, so you end up with anything but a true democracy.

CK, sales manager (corporate firm),
45, male, state education (left school at 16)

9   **How could the taxation system be made fairer; should we have inheritance tax?**

There should be a flat rate of tax to make the system fairer. Inheritance tax is double taxation and is totally unfair. Capital gains tax that is not subject to cost indexation is a tax on inflation and also totally unfair.

MP, chairman of top FTSE
100 international business, 65, male

I don't believe that there should be such a thing as inheritance tax as long as the assets are transferred to a family member. Assets left to non-family members should be taxed on the entire amount and given no relief at all. This would make the system fairer and I believe far simpler for HMRC to manage!

PS, city stockbroker,
34, male, privately educated

The taxation system should be made fairer and extensively overhauled. The whole system should be made simpler, cutting out in the process all the existing tax loopholes. No offshore nonsense. No tax benefits to trusts. Taking steps to reduce the

*black economy. Gains from 'short selling' and similar activities
which for some reason aren't taxed should be. I know this is
classed as gambling, but I believe all income from gambling of,
say, £1,000 or more should be taxed as income and any losses
could not be offset against gains. In my view it is immoral for
somebody to win many millions simply by choosing six numbers
and get it tax-free. I think the idea put forward amongst others by
the Liberal Democrats that rich people should pay at least a certain
percentage of their income in tax is excellent. As the average hard
working family pays about 20 per cent of their income in tax,
it would seem reasonable that anybody with an income of over
£150,000 should have a minimum tax bill of 20 per cent of their
income. As for inheritance tax, those with assets above the tax
threshold believe it's their money and they should be completely
free to do what they like with it. Unless they won it in a lottery
they have after all paid tax already. Then there are those who
don't have a large inheritance who believe it is unfair for others to
inherit. I believe inheritance tax should be abolished.*

JP, retired civil servant, 69, male,
first class honours degree in engineering

*The taxation system is always going to be inherently unfair; you
can't tax on income levels without looking at everyone's personal
circumstances. To make the system fairer everyone's personal tax
code should be calculated on a more detailed basis rather than
broad scales that do not take any other benefits or allowances
into consideration. For instance, if you have a couple with two
incomes and they own a home on a repayment mortgage and have
two children, one at nursery and one at school, and have parents
who are no longer working and are of pensionable age, they
should have any tax credits, children's credits, child-care credits
etc taken into account before they start paying income tax. The
level of personal income before income tax is deductible should be
much higher in many instances. Inheritance tax should ideally be
abolished; I don't understand the justification of deducting such*

*a high level of tax when the estate being left would have been
purchased from an income where tax has already been deducted.
I simply don't understand the need other than another route to
collect tax from someone who is no longer able to argue!*

SR, single mum/self-employed business owner, 36, female

*Inheritance tax is the most unjust of all taxes, scrap it. First of
all one needs to sort out HMRC, it is not fit for purpose. Now
look at tax in general. Most of the taxes we have today, direct and
indirect, did not exist in 1900. In 1900 we were the wealthiest
and most powerful nation on earth. I conclude with my already
stated point, the state should have a few core responsibilities; the
rest is the responsibility of the individual. Tax reduced from
£540 billion to £100 billion. It will happen but not for another
hundred years. Council tax, when council CEOs get paid more
than the prime minister, well – it is just a disgrace.*

GH, drainage cleaner, male,
37, honours degree, privately educated

*If I could answer this one, I would be a lot wealthier than
I am now! I firmly believe that it's right that everyone pays their
share, with perhaps a sliding scale based on annual salary, rather
than the step changes we currently have. Why not go up by
percentage points, so if you fall within a certain bracket you pay
27 per cent, just over that bracket you contribute 28 per cent and
so on and so forth. I don't think inheritance tax is a fair tax, as
the old adage says it's already been taxed once. However,
I imagine this is already costed into the nation's future budgets
so the bigger question should be, 'what would you replace it
with?' For the record I'm not sure of the answer but the obvious
answer of collecting all taxes due from business should be
a no-brainer.*

CK, sales manager (corporate firm),
45, male, state education (left school at 16)

Taxation needs to recognized by the public as something they are choosing to pay in order to live in the type of country they want: if they want medical care free at the point of delivery they must pay for it by working and paying tax. Likewise for education, transport, etc. Once this is taken on board by the general public there will be less objection to it being 'imposed on us' by those in power. Likewise, those who have plenty of money will not feel that they should try to get away with paying as little as possible. Everyone needs to be able to feel that they are part of the public who benefit from living in this type of society. Life is never fair – some people are born with sporting bodies, great beauty, high mental capacities, etc and others are less well endowed by nature. Animals have to live with what nature has dished out to them, whereas humans have the power to improve on nature. Taxation is just one way in which human societies can try to overcome the unfairness of nature. If the society thinks that no one should benefit from what their parents did, rather than from their own efforts , then inheritance tax will be the norm. If, however, the society feels that everyone must pay for their own way in life, then it will be a society which does not want to help weaker, less able people in it and benefits will not be given to the idle, or to the unhealthy who cannot work, and inheritance tax would never be allowed. The big question is: what kind of society do we want?

JC, retired religious education teacher,
69, female, public sector

10 Should anyone who was not born in the UK be allowed to claim UK benefits?

Only if such persons revoke their other citizenship and marry or permanently settle in the UK. However, such people should not have arrived in the first place without bringing in some skill or benefit to the economy.

MP, chairman of top FTSE
100 international business, 65, male

*Yes. If you come and work here when the native
population don't want the work and you then get made
redundant or have children, then yes. What I would do is
tighten up the NHS. You have been in the country less than
12 months: you have to pay the first £1,000 of your treatment
even if you are paying tax and NI. 12 to 24 months: first
£500, but you can reduce this by making a higher voluntary
NI contribution.*

GH, drainage cleaner, male,
37, honours degree, privately educated

*Not immediately, no. I think that economic migrants are
responsible for additional burdens on the state and the
taxpayers and this is unfair. Whilst it would be wonderful to
believe that in a Utopian state, every person would have access
to a better lifestyle, the simple answer is that they are not.
As such, I have no problem with migration if it's to work, but
to simply turn up and claim benefits is wrong. There should be
qualifying criteria to gain benefits. For examples, they must have
been resident in the UK and paying NI for (say) three years
before they can claim and then there should be limits placed on
the maximum paid.*

CK, sales manager (corporate firm),
45, male, state education (left school at 16)

*This is a daft suggestion – place of birth is irrelevant.
Your English mother might have been in Timbuktu on holiday
when she gave birth to you and at two days old you returned to
the family home and have lived and worked there ever since.
Place of work and home-base is the key. If you pay tax/have paid
tax/intend to pay tax, that is the basic position that might allow
you to claim benefits.*

JC, retired religious education teacher,
69, female, public sector

*If you were not born in the UK and are not a resident of the
UK then you should not be able to claim benefit. If you are a
resident of the UK and have contributed to the state's purse by
paying tax then you should be able to claim if you qualify – which
should be monitored far more strictly than it is currently. We have
far too many people in this country that are on a free ride!*

PS, city stockbroker,
34, male, privately educated

*Simply put, no for someone who has chosen to come here,
but equally there are instances where some benefits should be
offered (but not UK benefits). The ideal situation would be that
they are eligible to claim benefits from the country where they
were born. If there is no benefits system or they are genuine
refugees escaping from dangerous situations there should be a
system in place where they get some assistance but not the same
assistance offered to UK citizens. The benefits offered to those
not born in the UK should reflect the contribution made to
the economy historically by the individual and/or previous
generations of the family.*

SR, single mum/self-employed
business owner, 36, female

*If they have contributed to the UK economy then I feel that there
should be scope for some sort of benefit payment should the need
arise, though with strict controls and a limit on the amount of
time that these benefits could be paid.*

HS, British diplomatic community member,
45, male, lives in Belgium

Only UK citizens should be allowed to claim UK benefits.

JP, retired civil servant, 69, male,
first class honours degree in engineering

The generation gap

1 Do you feel proud of your generation?

No, I'm very ashamed of it. Despite the unprecedented drain on our resources of the Second World War by the mid-1960s we were a nation of wealth and power, whereas now we have little power, little wealth and a huge debt. Individually we have more wealth, a better standard of living and much increased comfort, but this has been achieved by greed and at the expense of what we can pass on to the next generations. They will not have the benefit of the sale of council houses or the sale of the nationalized industries or indeed the sale of much of our gold. They will not be able to benefit from the capitalization of the building societies. They will not have free university education, free dental care or even free planning and building regulation submissions. They will not inherit the wealth from North Sea oil and gas, that's all nearly gone. Instead, we have encumbered future generations by mortgaging their future with private finance initiatives where they are saddled with annual costs because we were not prepared to pay for it now. You could write a book on the huge number of stealth taxes that have been introduced over the years yet we get less and less for these taxes. I believe my generation of politicians has made two catastrophic blunders. The first was to allow such extensive immigration which has changed beyond redemption the whole culture and beliefs of the country, and with the higher birth rates among immigrants this is only going to get worse. At no time did the people vote for this and in my view this has introduced incalculable problems for future generations. It was done with very misguided good intentions. The second is the privatization of our assets, which despite my being a conservative, is proving to be an organizational and expensive disaster.

JP, retired civil servant, 69, male,
first class honours degree in engineering

I'm certainly not embarrassed by my generation.
Leaving school when we did when the country had record
unemployment and prospects were bleaker than they are now,
things have not turned out too bad, in my opinion. However,
I'm not 100 per cent sure if this is unique to my generation, but
there are certainly those who have lived off of benefits for the
majority of their adult life, which is horrific. At the other end of
the spectrum, many of those from my generation are those who
were Yuppies and are probably more responsible than others for
the present economic crisis. In summary, whilst I don't think any
generation is perfect, we've not dealt too badly with what we
have faced to date.

CK, sales manager (corporate firm),
45, male, state education (left school at 16)

No. My generation has not been strong enough to resist 'political
correctness' and has presided over a general deterioration of
personal standards and manners. For the most part we have
allowed educational standards to fall. We seem unable to
discipline wayward children. We have allowed minorities to
change our way of life. We have embraced the consumer society
without having any regard to the effects on the sustainability of
our planet. In other words, we have made a bit of a pig's breakfast
of our responsibilities.

MP, chairman of top FTSE
100 international business, 65, male

In some regard my generation has moved the economy and the
country on leaps and bounds, in other ways I feel my generation
is the lazy generation where benefits cheats, ambulance chasers
and greedy business leaders have monopolized the news. Actually
I come from the generation of the mobile phone (not the mobile
brick), online shopping really taking hold, huge growth in the
economy (before we scaled it back through the newest recession),

the increase in awareness of human rights, and the blossoming of many entrepreneurs.

SR, single mum/self-employed business owner, 36, female

Not at any point do I feel proud of my generation! The gang culture and the inherent laziness of some of my generation are leading to the downfall of our fine country. Whatever happened to common decency where if you saw someone in trouble then you would lend a hand? We are now a nation of responsibility dodgers that buck-pass at every corner of society. The gang culture that thrives in our inner cities is a cancer that is fast becoming terminal unless as a nation we address the core reasons for such a culture. We need to give school leavers incentives to get a job by increasing the amount of jobs that are available... the apprentice scheme should be a major priority to allow these disadvantaged people a chance to take responsibility for their lives and stop blaming the other classes and politicians for their plight!

PS, city stockbroker, 34, male, privately educated

No.

GH, drainage cleaner, male,
37, honours degree, privately educated

In some ways yes – we have lived through the poverty and pressure of war and post-war times, we have developed a country that tries to treat the handicapped as equals, we have tried to overcome huge class divisions and have tried to give sexual equality. We have stopped hanging offenders, we have tried to allow gay people to be gay, we have tried to spread education to all sorts of people. On the other hand, we have damaged our countryside in order to produce cheap food, to feed people who are getting obese, we have made machines to do the work that many less able people used to do and have therefore made them feel useless and in fact unemployed/unemployable, we have failed to give our young moral guidance, setting before them only the ambition to be rich, we have taught our young to be concerned for their own wellbeing before the needs of others. We admire 'fame' and famous show-offs instead of people of real worth who serve their fellow humans.

JC, retired religious education teacher,
69, female, public sector

Yes. My particular generation was probably the first that was made aware that it was a competitive marketplace for both goods and services as well as in the workplace. The 1980s saw a reinvention of the UK economy and whilst the death of the old and the birth of the new economy was painful, it was necessary. This gave the UK an initial advantage and allowed it to adapt quickly to changing events. Am I proud to be part of this generation? Yes.

HS, British diplomatic community member,
45, male, lives in Belgium

2 **Do you own anything made by Apple; if so how much of an impact does this corporate company have on your life every day?**

No, not yet. But I will – and very soon!

JP, retired civil servant, 69, male,
first class honours degree in engineering

I own an iPad, iPod, iPhone and Apple TV, so I have a large amount of my life affected by this corporate giant! The music that we own, the films that we watch, are all supplied to my household by Apple and on a more day-to-day basis my whole business and personal life is run from my iPhone. The phone allows me to see the weather, my diary, all of my work e-mails on the move and I would go as far as to say that my phone is the single most important accessory to my life! Apple is THE company of my generation and has progressed technology infinitely faster and left other technology companies in its wake!

PS, city stockbroker, male, 34, privately educated

Apple products (and primarily its late founder) are the classic example of brilliant, simple and very clever marketing. I, like most people (graphic designers excluded), had no need for Apple products, but then some electronics were given a makeover and became desirable. Apple products need no instruction manual and very quickly objects about which only months previously one said, 'What's the point of that?' became 'I can't live without my iPhone, iPad etc.' Brilliant and simple marketing.

HS, British diplomatic community member,
45, male, lives in Belgium

Yes. We cannot blame Apple per se. The technology would have been developed by others if not by Apple. The impact is however substantial and has changed the method and, more importantly, the speed of communication and information gathering forever. The development of the internet and IT generally is probably the most important change to our lives ever except perhaps the internal combustion engine.

MP, chairman of top FTSE
100 international business, 65, male

Certainly not. The iPhone looks horrid and far too complicated to use. The iPad and iPod are things I have no interest in at all. I like to engage with life, hear, see, and experience the sounds and sights of the city or the quiet village. I could think of nothing worse than listening to music whilst out and about. More importantly is the impact it has on my day-to-day life. Cyclists with iPods? This demonstrates the sheer stupidity that now affects at least 50 per cent of the populace. These are the same people who stand the moment an aircraft lands, the same people who drive in fog without fog lights, the same people who when their car breaks down either don't put out a warning triangle or the even more stupid who do and place it one yard behind the car. Just think: as the HGV approaches, what does he see first – the 5ft-wide Ford Focus with flashing hazards or the

12-inch-wide triangle sitting a yard behind the bumper?
I rest my case. Now throw into the equation the iPod user who
plays music so loud on the train or tube you can hear it coming
through their headphones even if you suffered from deafness.
These people must know that the music can be heard. So why do
they not just bring some speakers with them. I'd much rather hear
the music than some beating drone. This symbolizes the ignorance,
stupidity and selfishness that now defines our nation. I once heard
an urban myth that there was a chap on South Eastern trains,
a commuter, who carried with him a pair of nail scissors.
If someone was playing their music too loudly, on getting off at
his stop and assuming the offender had their eyes closed, he
would snip the wire from the iPod to the headphones and then
knock on the window as the train pulled out of the station and
wave his scissors at the individual who was frantically pressing
buttons on the iPod as they had no idea why their music had
ceased. Give that man a knighthood.

GH, drainage cleaner, male,
37, honours degree, privately educated

I do own Apple products and to my eternal shame, I would have
to say I cannot get through a day without multiple uses of some
of their devices, in particular the iPhone and iPad. It has enabled
me to do so much more but I couldn't quantify whether the
'more' I'm doing is enhancing my day greatly. Why Apple? Well I
have always been a sucker for a brand and they have capitalized
brilliantly on this across the globe, creating a want and a need for
more Apple products. An incredible story really and emblematic of
the material possessions demanded by society in general.

CK, sales manager (corporate firm),
45, male, state education (left school at 16)

I have an Apple phone and cannot imagine how I lived without it
now. I am now fully reliant on Apple looking after all my personal
everyday data from calendar appointments to telephone numbers,

e-mail addresses and everything in between. Slightly concerning
when you look at the information that is now collated in one
place and in the hands of a corporate organization.

SR, single mum/self-employed
business owner, 36, female

NO, none.

JC, retired religious education teacher,
69, female, public sector

3   **Should the UK debt crisis have ever happened and who was to**
    blame?

Definitely not. Our politicians are to blame and in particular the
last Labour government with Gordon Brown playing the biggest
part in the scandal. During the economic 'good times' when he
was chancellor we should have been building up reserves. We
should not have been throwing money at the NHS and other
organizations merely to gain political favour with the public.
If only we had built up a surplus when we were selling our silver
(national assets) and gold (literally) and had something to show
for the North Sea oil and gas bonanza. If only we had paid our
way with higher taxes to meet our spending commitments and
been more prudent we could have amassed a large surplus.
We should also never have allowed the welfare and benefit costs
to have risen so extensively and we should also never have
allowed so many quangos to be created. This would mean we
wouldn't now be paying huge interest on the debt and could
have interest paid to us on a surplus. If we had behaved more
financially prudently it is very likely the banking crisis would
have been considerably less traumatic. As a country we have
still contributed less to bail out the banks than Gordon Brown
borrowed in the year before the banking crisis.

JP, retired civil servant, 69, male,
first class honours degree in engineering

The problem of debt began because greedy people encouraged the ignorant to borrow money for things and homes which they had no hope of ever paying back. This lending was not done in order to enable the poor to enter a nicer lifestyle, but simply because a profit could be made from them taking on the loans. The debt crisis grew and grew because no one in power had the courage to contradict what was happening, although it was obviously doomed to failure just to borrow for the benefit of now (beautiful hospitals, lovely schools, posh new shopping centres, etc) with no regard to the future effects – who will pay for all this when the money lenders want their money back in order to realize their profits.

JC, retired religious education teacher,
69, female, public sector

It is a real shame that the debt crisis took hold. More self-awareness and a little restraint in investment decisions might have kept us in a more stable and strong position when the crisis started. Perhaps an element of the right hand knowing what the left hand is doing may have also averted the crisis but perhaps it had to happen to ensure we as a country took stock and stabilized our position through a recession, so we can start to grow slowly again and regain our financial position. Who was to blame? America! Lack of ability to communicate about problems meant their decisions forced us into a position without any preparation.

SR, single mum/self-employed business owner, 36, female

Now the full facts have been revealed it seems inevitable that there would be a UK debt crisis. The blame lies solely at the feet of the UK government and the FSA and the now infamous 'light touch regulation'. I can imagine that finance (being our biggest industry at the time) and the revenues it was creating for the government was quite a seductive partner but to let it go on unheeded was only going to head one way. An economy where people were able to borrow up to four, maybe five times, their annual salary is in a very precarious position. For the FSA to be hamstrung by the government was criminal and for them not to raise the spectre of a crash was untenable by them. Part of the problem you could say is that the industry's regulating authority, the FSA, was staffed by people who were executives from the very companies they are supposed to be regulating. Conflict of interest anyone?

CK, sales manager (corporate firm),
45, male, state education (left school at 16)

The debt crisis that we are trying to crawl out of currently is a global issue and has affected each and every developed economy; there are many places to point blame; however, I am yet to be convinced that there is one specific event that can be held responsible for the whole issue. The original issue came about when the ratings agencies issued packaged debt products (sub-prime) as creditworthy and created a time bomb that linked each financial entity and this in my opinion was the beginning of the world's issues! The UK specifically couldn't isolate itself from the crisis as we have state and corporate ties to Europe; the blame for the issues in Greece, Portugal, Spain and Italy lie with the Eurozone welcoming in countries that were not suitable to be in a single currency.

PS, city stockbroker, 34, male, privately educated

The debt crisis isn't a UK problem, it is a global worry. But what has happened is that credit dried after the collapse and saving of the banking sector and the wake-up call happened. An advantage that the UK has is that it can still count on a central bank that is able to react to a given situation and not (like the ECB) a central bank that has to look and create policies for 17 different countries that won't have the same impact in each. As far as who is to blame for the crisis, it has to be everyone. A very trite comment sure, but basic home management teaches us not to live over our means and

*to prepare for a rainy day, because at some point, those clouds will
pass over and, it will rain.*

HS, British diplomatic community member,
45, male, lives in Belgium

*In a perfect society, it should not have happened. The cause was
pure greed both by the provider and the recipient of easy money.*

MP, chairman of top FTSE
100 international business, 65, male

*Well of course it should never have happened. Who was
to blame? The evil, greedy and lazy bankers of course! Or were
they? Watch any debate on the issue and the argument is so
boring and ill informed. Politicians of all persuasions blame
'bankers'. Politicians blame other politicians. Joe Public blames
bankers and to an extent politicians, but most are so poorly
educated they neither understand the argument nor care.
And then there is the person who was actually to blame.
Gordon Brown? No. Fred Goodwin? No. His name was John
Smith and not the former Labour politician, but the average
member of the once Great British Public. Banks were stupid,
nay, idiotic to offer such credit to the average man and woman,
but no one forced that person to punch in their pin number and
purchase a £1,000 plasma TV when their disposable income
was only £250 per month. Good housekeeping was the order
of the day in the 1950s, wage packets came on a Friday, in
cash and were handed over to the woman of the house for
'housekeeping'. If she had £70, that was what she knew she
could spend, not £71, not £96, but £70. Live for the moment,
spend now, pay later was the order of the day, for politicians
and the general public alike. Looking back, it was a catastrophe
waiting to happen. Families spending four months' disposable
income on a week's holiday. Not sustainable. Never was and
I was saying this 10 years ago, whilst running up my own huge
personal debt. Friday night, cash machine, credit card, 10 crisp*

*£10 notes which meant three £1 coins as an increase in the
minimum payment next month, no contest. So where are we
now? In a position of no hope. We blame lack of growth on
people not spending in the shops, but this is exactly how we
bombed in the first place, so the way to recovery is to make the
same mistake again. I apologize for not quite comprehending
this insanity. And now apparently the deficit cuts, according to
some people, are not necessary. We spend £680 billion from
government and take £540 billion in tax. Try going to fill up with
petrol (if you can afford to), putting in £80 of unleaded and then
saying to the attendant, 'I've only got £60, ok with you'. Just try
it and see what happens.*

GH, drainage cleaner, male,
37, honours degree, privately educated

4 Do we live in a blame culture?

*If the law had remained available for the poor to use there would
not have been the growth of lawyers who use the no-win, no-fee
system. This makes everyone feel it's worth having a go. The result
is people want to blame others, because they hope they may be
able to make money for their case, rather than accept blame for
their share in the cause of the accident. In fact, the lawyers advise
you never to accept the blame.*

JC, retired religious education teacher,
69, female, public sector

*I believe we do live in a blame culture and it saddens me.
We need business to be able to take risks without employees
fearing for their livelihoods. Risk certainly needs to be managed
but industry is littered with examples where initiatives have
been launched but in a half-baked way. If you're going to
do something, commit to it 100 per cent so you're never left
wondering. Also, some of the blame must lie with individuals
who seem afraid of attracting any criticism. Constructive criticism*

*can be a force for good and should be embraced as such and not
shied away from.*

> CK, sales manager (corporate firm),
> 45, male, state education (left school at 16)

*Yes. It is an indication that whatever the cause of a problem,
someone else is responsible. Taken to its limit, it will result in
nobody doing anything in case they get the blame.*

> MP, chairman of top FTSE
> 100 international business, 65, male

*Yes. Encouraged by a greedy legal profession too eager to make
money by finding culprits, where perhaps none exist. This has
been allowed to develop because too many of our politicians
come from the legal profession.*

> JP, retired civil servant,
> 69, male, first class honours degree in engineering

*Last time I looked we were. I smoke, I drink, if I get admitted
to hospital with kidney cancer and the surgeon after a long
week removes the wrong kidney and I die, well if my parents
sued the NHS I would turn in my grave. I chose that way of
life. My fault. Look at whiplash claims. Just shocking. I had a
very serious sporting injury, people said I should sue the player
involved, the hospital for incompetence (and my, were they
incompetent), but that is life, shit happens, accidents happen.
In the words of Lieutenant Dempsey from the great 1980s police
show* Dempsey and Makepeace, *'life is hard, then you die'.*

> GH, drainage cleaner, male,
> 37, honours degree, privately educated

*I am afraid that we do! We live in a culture where responsibility
no longer holds a place at the top table and this is a fundamental
flaw to our society. From bad calls at work to excuses at
home we no longer put our hands up and admit fault. If we*

stopped for a minute and began to take responsibility for our actions I believe that our country would regenerate back to its former glory where the rest of the world looks to the British as a great nation!

PS, city stockbroker,
34, male, privately educated

Yes – I blame lots of people and countries for lots of bad things! If I do I guess we all do!

SR, single mum/self-employed
business owner, 36, female

No, I think we live in a culture where dreams have been sold and where we feel it is our right to seek justice. Unfortunately even this is now a lucrative business opportunity with the likes of 'We'll Take Them To The Cleaners & Partners' with a 'no-win, no-fee' marketing that has led people to believe that it's worth a punt to take on an apparent wrong-doer because a paving stone had moved a couple of millimetres and a toe had been stubbed. Someone taught me that 'when we point the finger of blame, there are three fingers pointing straight back' (try it) and this I feel can also be said for the present tough times.

HS, British diplomatic community member,
45, male, lives in Belgium

5   **Has all the IT progression improved the way people communicate and keep in touch or has it stopped real conversations?**

I don't think it has changed conversations but it has changed the method of written communications. A new language is being developed which, in itself, is no bad thing as languages have developed over the centuries. I think it is sad that letter-writing appears to be a thing of the past and that proper grammar is obsolete. I am surprised by the lack of knowledge of punctuation even by senior people in the company. On balance

*communication has improved but the methods are difficult for
older people to assimilate.*

MP, chairman of top FTSE
100 international business, 65, male

*It has made communication easier and quicker and should
have improved communication greatly. However, because
of the ease of sending e-mail to so many people at once, the
volume generated has become counter-productive with the
important lost amongst the rubbish. Texting has not helped good
communication; if texts had been around before the ability to
actually talk to people on the phone, the latter would have been
hailed as a great development.*

JP, retired civil servant, 69, male,
first class honours degree in engineering

*I think the way we communicate has been improved by
technology many fold. It is now easier than ever in history
to communicate with friends, family etc and that can only be
a good thing. I imagine this question was being asked when
Alexander Graham Bell invented the telephone but that only
enhanced people's communication and the modern-day
IT revolution should be seen in the same light. The one
thing that could be levelled at today's communication is
that it can be seen as intrusive. It is all-pervasive and it's
sometimes a struggle to keep everyone's full attention
(whether at work or socially) with people forever checking
smart phones etc.*

CK, sales manager (corporate firm),
45, male, state education (left school at 16)

*Communication has clearly been made easier than it was when
people needed to go out and find a phone booth with a working
phone, or wait for letters to arrive. However, speedy methods
of communication sometimes means that people don't give*

themselves time to think before communicating. IT is a very mixed blessing.

JC, retired religious education teacher,
69, female, public sector

In a word? Yes! With the advent of social networks and before that mobile text messages, we tend to be more engaged with old mates that we haven't spoken to for 20 years than seeing what's happening at home. It's become pretty sad that people now talk of 'weaning themselves off of social networks' (mea culpa) but on a positive side services that use VoIP have allowed greater communication and let families stay in touch. This surely must be seen as positive.

HS, British diplomatic community member,
45, male, lives in Belgium

Some technology adds a huge amount of value to the way that people can communicate! I can now speak to my sister in Australia via my television and see her on the screen which allows us to stay in touch far better than just a telephone call… it allows her to see her nieces whenever she likes, even living on the other side of the planet! Where technology has taken something from our society is children are now able to play video games online with each other and as such no longer have to leave their rooms to communicate with their friends! It is sad because the social skills that they are losing by locking themselves away will inevitably hamper them in their adult lives.

PS, city stockbroker, 34, male, privately educated

Forget the tobacco companies, e-mail is the devil! We no longer chat, we text and we no longer pick up the phone for business contacts but drop them an e-mail so we don't interrupt our day. We have to add smiley faces, speak in a techno-language, and put kisses at the end of everything. Our intended communication often gets misread which leads to numerous additional texts and e-mails being sent to confirm our interpretation of a single line communication which has considerable cost and environmental impact. Just pick up the phone!

SR, single mum/self-employed
business owner, 36, female

This is progress. Would you prefer the modern communications of 2012 or the fax and the brick phone of 1988? Modern communications are like any development when the question, 'how did we live without...' is asked. People lived without TV, they lived without cars, and they even lived without toilets. Yes, it is nice every so often to put pen to paper and write a letter and even with a fountain pen, but e-mail, phone, Skype and the like are invariably better than a phone box, telegrams and a carrier pigeon. However, there are some major downsides. In 1990 you could go on holiday and unless you left a forwarding hotel address you could return two weeks later to find your house had burnt down, your car had been stolen and your entire share portfolio had been wiped as you had decided to invest massively in Barings Bank. Today you can be trying to relax on holiday and take a call from your neighbour saying that your security light in your garden came on last night or that your side gate was open. Well, you are 5,000 miles away in Florida, what exactly are you going to do? Additionally, senior executives and indeed middle management can never relax as the dreaded Blackberry beeps as they ascend a ski lift. They fear that they have to be seen to still be in touch with HQ. Too many decisions were probably made during the years that preceded the credit crunch by these very people, under pressure, on holiday and not with the full information to hand when making decisions. This is a massive negative impact that needs to be addressed. Children with mobiles, some families have five phones, and children aged 11, 12 and even younger have a mobile. Bonkers, and an extra drain on tight family incomes. One thing IT hasn't affected is the pointless meetings that are held routinely in large companies, meetings to discuss meetings, these 'real' conversations still

*continue whatever the dominance of the new world of modern
communications, but they are as time-wasting and useless as
they always have been and compliance and HR must shoulder
much of the blame.*

GH, drainage cleaner, male,
37, honours degree, privately educated

6   Is the world too worried about offending people?

*Rightly so, we should be concerned about offending people,
but equally we should be entitled to speak openly about our
views. It is human nature to want to avoid hurting or offending
someone but there is an element of political correctness on
what is considered offensive. I would like to think I am of
reasonable intelligence and although there is the odd moment
of putting one's foot in one's mouth when speaking to someone
I would not openly make comments that I know are likely to
cause offence.*

SR, single mum/self-employed
business owner, 36, female

*Yes. There is too much influence from vocal minorities. Political
correctness has gone too far. It is inevitable that eventually the
silent majority will arise and the effects of that could be much
more damaging than dealing with the problem now. The opinions
of the legislators are out of tune with the vast majority.*

MP, chairman of top FTSE
100 international business, 65, male

*Most definitely, you can't please all of the people all of the time
and I don't know why this has become redundant in society. I am
not saying that we should allow people to regress and have the
freedom to abuse the minority or the weak. What I am saying is
that what makes us great as a race is that we are all different and
to that notion we will not always see eye to eye; this is not a bad*

*thing as if we all thought the same and saw the world in the same
light then it would be a very boring existence!*

PS, city stockbroker,
34, male, privately educated

*Quite simply, yes. Instead of becoming more sophisticated
and more tolerant as we evolve, we seem to be taking backward
steps. If you think about cartoons about the Prophet Mohammed
resulting in death threats and protests, if you think about the
barriers now put on humour for fear of offending anyone, about
a teacher being unable to offer constructive criticism to a child,
then yes, we are becoming far too delicate. Now, I wouldn't
condone people offending others for their beliefs etc, but there
needs to be a level of common decency and common sense in the
reaction to these areas. Quite simply, not everyone will agree with
everyone. Don't you agree?*

CK, sales manager (corporate firm),
45, male, state education (left school at 16)

*I think that the media is so direct now that one has to be extra
careful about what one does and says. Administrations give
guidelines on how to deal in any given situation so as not to send
out the wrong message or to cause offence. The media too has its
part to play (yet again) for comments that previously would have
been chuckled at now get thrust into the limelight. I think of the
example of Jeremy Clarkson on BBC's* The One Show *making
comments on the striking public sector workers, with the show's
hosts obviously receiving instructions through their earpieces
being told to apologize and squirming on the sofa. The media
latched onto this and from a few people with no sense of humour
and nothing better to do than to call and hope to speak to Anne
Robinson at the BBC, to creating a witch-hunt and trying to stir
public opinion.*

HS, British diplomatic community member,
45, male, lives in Belgium

Yes, and many people are too easily offended, particularly ethnic minorities.

JP, retired civil servant, 69, male,
first class honours degree in engineering

Depends where in the world you live in. Frankie Boyle doesn't seem to care; Iran's crazed president doesn't seem to care. Yes, there will always be the barmy brigade from Brent or the Green Party who jump up and down and claim offensive comments from Jeremy Clarkson mean he should be sacked. Just get on with it. Life is too short.

GH, drainage cleaner, male,
37, honours degree, privately educated

No. Everyone should worry about causing offence to anyone. This question is based on the dislike of PC speech. People can go over the top on imposing political correctness, but without it we used to be horrible to one another and the weak had no way of resisting the bullying and unkindness. As long as PC rules are applied intelligently they are a good thing.

JC, retired religious education teacher,
69, female, public sector

7   In the world of Google and social media, does the 'twelve-man jury' still have a place in our legal system; can you get truly uninfluenced opinions or is there a better solution?

We have to trust in the twelve-man jury system because the other option is a judge making his own decision. The only way to decide on a person's future is to get a joint opinion from a (hopefully) neutral diverse snapshot of society.

PS, city stockbroker, 34, male, privately educated

The ordinary 'person' is generally much better informed than he/she is given credit for. Prior to Google etc opinions were influenced by books, journals, lectures, education etc. I see no difference to that form of opinion-making to the present social media. I can think of no better system than the twelve-man jury.

MP, chairman of top FTSE
100 international business, 65, male

Even before the internet I believe the jury system was far from perfect and that in many complex cases the average person is just not qualified to make a correct verdict. It has always struck me that the legal profession flatter themselves by the rigid assumption that the verdict of the jury is correct. Unless of course it can make money from appeals. The jury system is clearly inappropriate for complicated fraud and tax cases. I was on the panel of prospective jury members for a lengthy VAT fraud trial. I had lost all interest before the long list of charges had been read out. Luckily I wasn't called; I really would have had difficulty keeping awake for the three-week trial. If we must have this human rights nonsense then surely forcing somebody to do jury service against their will is an infringement of such rights.

JP, retired civil servant, 69, male,
first class honours degree in engineering

Most individuals who are called for jury service would agree that it can be difficult to judge a case solely on the facts in front of you when you are easily influenced by public opinion which is so readily available. The ideal of having a jury is great but in cases which are complex in nature and when political opinions are so blatant now, perhaps a new system should be implemented.

SR, single mum/self-employed
business owner, 36, female

One hopes that any kind of dumbing down of the legal system is not even a possibility. There can be nothing more frightening than imagining a Google search on possible sentences and precedents during a trial. But is it such a far-off possibility?

Didn't the tabloids virtually act as judge and jury following
the murder of Bristol landscape architect, Jo Yeates? They latched
onto her landlord, Christopher Jefferies and virtually conducted
a trial through their front pages. Trials are emotive at any time
and one just hopes that independence is assured, but this has
always been the risk. So in all honesty, one hopes that the
'twelve-man jury' will remain the trusted method of the legal
system.

HS, British diplomatic community member,
45, male, lives in Belgium

Once upon a time the jury were the local neighbours and
everyone knew everyone, and all the rumours about the case
that were going around. Under Google, it is still the same.
There is no solution. Judges can try their best to direct the jury to
deal only with what they have heard in the court, but no one has
'uninfluenced' opinions as we all have our own prejudices
(eg women drivers are not as good as men, so she is clearly
guilty; he's black so he shouldn't be over here, hence he is the
guilty one, etc). Cases could be better done if ALL the facts
were known about a suspect, such as what previous cases he
had been involved in, what prison record does he have, rather
than the present system of only telling the jury about the present
case in hand. When the jury find they have freed a bad man
and convicted an innocent one because they were denied all the
facts they feel lied to and undervalued. Our legal system needs
other reforms long before it worries about juries googling for
information.

JC, retired religious education teacher,
69, female, public sector

I absolutely believe in the twelve-man jury system. Of the jury
being in the actual room with the accused and the witnesses etc.
I suppose the temptation could be to move these proceedings
online in the future but for me this would not be a progressive

*step for the justice system. With regards to whether opinions
can be influenced before and during a trial, from means other
than those in court, this is a very real danger. You could Google
the defendant's name and find previous newspaper clippings
(perhaps) or find them on Facebook and start to draw conclusions
that are not based on the evidence presented in court. The net
result being (one way or the other) that conclusions could be
drawn outside of the trial and this makes a mockery of it.
How to stop this? I imagine the only way would be to erase
(or hide) all reference to that person online for the duration of
the trial. With today's IT programs and systems, this should not
be beyond the wit of man.*

CK, sales manager (corporate firm),
45, male, state education (left school at 16)

*This is probably the most testing question of all and one could end
up writing a mini dissertation on it. This question tests the thought
process more than any other on the list. However, I will be brief.
Yes, emphatically yes. Innocent until proven guilty. The fool who
drives without his fog lights, he gets to sit on a jury as does the
cyclist with the iPod. No hope, but then something changes; their
idle 21st-century brains suddenly become focused, perhaps more
than ever in their lives. They have the future of a man or woman in
their hands. No silly motorway signs flashing 'have you prepared
your car for winter', treating us all with childish contempt, this
is as real as it gets. Rich, poor, black, white, socialist, Thatcherite,
all sitting to pass judgement on someone whose life could change
forever and, lest we not forget, the victim as well. A juror probably
learns more in that life-defining moment of responsibility than in
any other experience. Keep it, 100 per cent. I have faith that the
12 men and women can be independent, not influenced and in
most cases get the verdict right.*

GH, drainage cleaner, male,
37, honours degree, privately educated

8   How do we address the gap between rich and poor – and should we?

The main aim is to educate. Through education it is far easier to lift people out of a situation rather than trying to drag people into a situation. Rich and poor is such an emotive issue. I really don't think anyone has the definitive answer and it would be churlish of me to try and pretend that I do, apart from the fact that everyone deserves education, to be given a chance. Cop out? Possibly.

HS, British diplomatic community member,
45, male, lives in Belgium

Sadly there will always be a gap between rich and poor in our country because we have so many people not working! This can be addressed by allowing the rich, who are traditionally the wealth creators, to create new jobs in the UK and to make sure that we have trained workers ready to fill these roles. The wealth gap has grown because the past government leant too heavily on the City and allowed our manufacturing sector which was traditionally in the other areas of the UK to die. As a nation we need to work together in order to reverse this cycle and revive business in the less advantaged areas of the country!

PS, city stockbroker, 34, male, privately educated

Any successful economic entity has to have a gap between rich and poor. To try to deal with the gap would be wrong, as communist countries have experienced. It is much better to devise ways of making the rich spend their money which then filters down to the poorer members of society and to the government through consumption taxes.

MP, chairman of top FTSE
100 international business, 65, male

It's never been managed before and it won't happen in the future, therefore it's a moot point. There will always be rich and poor and rather than worrying about this gap, time would be better spent making sure the most vulnerable in society are looked after and the chance is there for all, if they've the will and the capabilities, to improve their own wealth. Developing nations around the world are now lifting up their gross GDP and as they do, there are more opportunities for all to improve their own situations. Despite some outdated ideologies, this is and will remain a capitalist global economy so there will never be equality in terms of wealth.

CK, sales manager (corporate firm),
45, male, state education (left school at 16)

There will always be a gap between rich and poor and other than becoming Robin Hood it will exist past our generation. We shouldn't necessarily hand over money to address the gap but provide better opportunities for those who have a limited income to address it themselves. Business opportunities are available to everyone willing to work, and if they are not willing to work to the best of their ability, then they should not complain. There are those that are working the current system of living through the benefits system whilst complaining that they are poor.

SR, single mum/self-employed
business owner, 36, female

The gap between rich and poor has become far too big and action must be taken to reduce it. Putting a stop to the rich finding ways round paying tax is a priority, the proposed initiative to make the 'intention' of tax laws overriding and make clever or devious interpretation of the small print to avoid tax no longer possible.

JP, retired civil servant, 69, male,
first class honours degree in engineering

Only animals have to accept life as it is dealt out to them by nature. Humans have the capacity to try to improve on nature. For example, humans use drugs to enable an animal to 'go to sleep' rather than suffer. Humans have the capacity to share

*their wealth so that poorer people do not have to suffer the
problems that poverty brings. Of course we ought to address
the gap between the rich and poor.*

JC, retired religious education teacher,
69, female, public sector

*Ask me this question in 1992 and I would say no. The left would
bleat that the gap between rich and poor was growing, evil Maggie
was to blame etc. But, just because the gap in the 1980s widened,
look more closely: 90 per cent got richer, so although the gap
widened, pretty much everyone was better off. Then something
happened. Firstly people began to believe life owed them a living
(me included), an explosion of magazines and TV programmes
encouraging the 'must-have society', 'I want, I want, I want' and
at the same time an explosion in what appears are profit-only
companies. We've always needed banks, oil companies, insurance
companies and so forth, but now it seems there are thousands and
thousands of people working in 'the City' who do things that earn
vast rewards for them and their employers, but if their companies
ceased to exist one Monday afternoon, what actual effect would
their demise have on the wider economy? Ok, tax may fall and
they may be on the dole queue, but would the economy grind to
a halt? I think not. You have an oil company go bust suddenly;
we may have no fuel to power our car. A bank goes bust, savers
lose their money. Tesco goes belly up, the corner shop is suddenly
having its shelves stripped of everything from tinned carrots to
Mazola cooking oil. But some of these companies in the City, no.
And it appears that it is these companies that seem to pay the most
money to people who have become so much wealthier than the rest
of the populace that a real envy has developed from those further
down the ladder. Chance of this ever changing – about as much as
MK Dons winning the UEFA Champions League.*

GH, drainage cleaner, male,
37, honours degree, privately educated

9 How do we correct the path of the next generation; does it need correcting?

Each generation, and especially now, is an evolution of the previous one. Personally I am old school and believe that respect for others is one of the most important aspects of guiding the next generation. But again this question is difficult to answer as I and my family have a fairly privileged life compared to most and my point of view might not be possible for those who have not had the same opportunities as myself. I believe that it is important to show the next generation that communicating is very important.

HS, British diplomatic community member,
45, male, lives in Belgium

Most of the next generation are decent pleasant kids. It is the minority, mainly from families where the emphasis is on living off benefits, who badly need correcting. Nobody should get taxpayers' money for nothing, even if it means they have to paint coal to earn it. We need to change the belief in so many that the world owes them a living. We need to scrap the human rights act and replace it with an act that spells rights for only those that have earned them, or at least have not forfeited them by bad behaviour.

JP, retired civil servant, 69, male,
first class honours degree in engineering

I'm not sure there is a path that needs correcting for the next generation. It would seem to be that education is more available than it ever has been and it's only through education (in all its guises) that progress is made. There has been no generation that's been perfect and I believe everything we know tells us that each generation over-achieves on the previous generation so I imagine we are in pretty safe hands here.

CK, sales manager (corporate firm),
45, male, state education (left school at 16)

*The next generation are probably better equipped to correct their
own path rather than having it dictated by older generations. If it is
to be corrected then this can only be achieved by better education.*

MP, chairman of top FTSE
100 international business, 65, male

*Certain aspects of the next generation will unfortunately become
the 'lost' generation; they will have to work for even longer
than us in order to pay for the debts that our nation is currently
generating. There will also be a wider wealth gap that in my
opinion can't be avoided as much of the next generation is already
disillusioned and will be perpetually unemployed!*

PS, city stockbroker, 34, male, privately educated

*'Education, education, education', the words of Tony Blair.
How does one explain the following? True poverty, not the
poverty we had in the 1860s, 1930s or 1960s where children died
of TB, were crippled by polio, wore rags and lived 10 to a room,
has effectively been eradicated. The school budget has increased
to record levels. Computers in schools, access to the wealth of
knowledge of the world wide web and of course smaller class
sizes. My grandmother had a class of 60 during the General Strike
of 1926 in Peckham, which has always, whatever you may have
heard, been, how do we say politely, not the nicest of areas.
My mother was at a standard south London primary, again in
an area of inner London as a pupil in the 1950s, as was my father.
Class size was 45. She has shown me her exercise books from
age 9. Hardly a spelling mistake with words such as 'translucent',
'mysterious' and so on. Whatever the politicians and educational
establishment may spout, educational standards are abysmal.
I have run a football team in the wealthy commuter belt of
Sevenoaks, not urban, deprived inner city London. Some of the
opposition players in their late teens and twenties I have faced
have barely been able to construct a basic sentence, after
10 years being educated by the state. Nothing short of a total*

*disgrace. There are so many aspects of education that are
wrong. Uniform. Breach the uniform code, send the child home.
Haircuts, breach the hair rules, send the child home. Lunches.
Jamie Oliver can try as much as he wants, things will never
change. Simple, one choice of meal, varied during the week, don't
like it, go hungry. Teachers should always wear gowns. Pupils
should always stand when a teacher enters a room. School days
extended to 4.30 pm. Exams. My father's O level Latin paper
was harder than my 1994 A level Latin paper. I will accept that
the introduction of coursework has been the correct approach,
but the percentage should be 20–25 per cent and should not be
able to be resubmitted. Exams are tough, life is tough, life is an
exam. You don't attend an interview for work, screw up and then
get a second chance to be re-interviewed. An interview for a job
is an exam and exams must be tougher and take precedence over
coursework and of course exam standards must be made harder.
What has happened to the U [unclassified/fail] grade? Failure is
part of life and if the mark is not good enough then a fail grade
must be awarded. Finally the leaving age should be reduced to
14, not raised to 18. Some people are not born academic; do not
waste their, the teacher's and the more able fellow pupils' time
by forcing these young people to sit, bored whilst their brains
sit idle. Get them out and into apprenticeships at 14. If you
can't read and write by 14, there is something seriously wrong.
Maths and English by this age, decent standards are what the
14-year-old leaver needs, not Shakespeare, astrophysics and who
was King of England in 1512. My grandmother said the only
people who couldn't read or write in her class of 60 were the
dumb, the deaf and the daft. Combine these changes with strict
discipline and we can make a start. If not the future generations
have no chance, the less academic will be failed and the academics,
the future neuro-surgeons, businessmen and engineers will have
their own development stunted.*

GH, drainage cleaner, male,
37, honours degree, privately educated

Each generation has been considered by the previous to have strayed from the path of the best way to behave and do things, but you have to let each generation learn from its own mistakes and correct things where needed. As a generation we need to support and have faith in the next generation just like parents with children.

SR, single mum/self-employed business owner, 36, female

Adults should seek to give a good example to the next generation. Adults should take responsibility for their own actions and the actions of their young.

JC, retired religious education teacher,
69, female, public sector

10 Should we tolerate gang culture or arm police and tackle it head on?

There is nothing wrong with gangs as long as their members behave themselves and don't misbehave or break the law in any way. I don't think there is any way we can prevent gangs forming. There are so many ways people can form into groups or gangs that they will always be around. At school we had the 'front drive gang' and the 'back drive gang' purely formed on the basis of which drive you walked to school down. Clearly we need and have some highly trained armed police, but I don't think it necessary or advisable to arm all police. Where we are going very wrong is to tolerate minor levels of criminal behaviour instead of having zero tolerance. In the short term this is going to require considerably more resources, but once the message gets out that any form of crime won't pay, then society will greatly benefit and costs of prison places etc will come down. Incidentally prison should be made a tougher and less attractive option. I think more effort should go into providing better opportunities for young people to do something constructive and fun. Examples are more scout and girl guide groups, more organized but informal sport, more choirs, and more amateur acting groups. There is one problem

*in that there will still be a number of individuals or gangs from
the benefit-dependent underclass that are just not up to doing
anything other than aimless messing around. For these perhaps
the reintroduction of national service is the answer.*

JP, retired civil servant, 69, male,
first class honours degree in engineering

*As it stands at the moment I totally disagree with arming our
police force. To me this is the slippery slope to worse and more
violent crime. If our police are armed, then it stands to reason
that our most violent criminals will do the same to even the
playing field. If by gang culture we are talking about feral youths
roaming the streets, causing mayhem and committing crimes,
then absolutely this should be stamped out. But what is a gang?
Is a group of 12 friends playing football up the park considered
a gang? Any individual or group of people going out with the
express intention to bring misery to others, to commit crime and
live outside the laws of a normal, accepted society should be
crushed at every opportunity. If to achieve this goal our police
need to be armed on a needs-must basis, that's fine, but we should
not unilaterally arm our police service.*

CK, sales manager (corporate firm),
45, male, state education (left school at 16)

*This is not a one or the other question. No, we shouldn't tolerate
gang culture but equally the answer is not a simple 'give police
guns to tackle it'. Gang culture, now that it has roots in our
community, would simply expand at a considerable rate if police
were armed and ready to tackle it. Suddenly it would take on
religious or human rights issues and before we know it, street
violence and turf wars would be breaking out. Gangs can only be
discouraged if better opportunities are offered than individuals
currently get. Look at what drives those that join gangs and see
how they can be engaged with.*

SR, single mum/self-employed business owner, 36, female

It would be impossible to get rid of 'gang culture'. Gangs are just an extension of clubs and societies. However, when they behave in a manner contrary to normal codes of conduct they should be tackled head on by the firmest means available.

MP, chairman of top FTSE
100 international business, 65, male

Operation Trident* may be disbanded. Why? Rumours are that it is wrong to have a police unit dedicated to one racial group. However much I may yearn for the sound of willow on leather in a 1950s English village, cream teas and a bobby with a truncheon and a whistle, we are living in 2012. 12-year-olds in Manchester with guns, gangsters with machine guns and an ever present terrorist threat. All police should be armed, but if this is restricted to metropolitan centres or even just London, Liverpool, Manchester, Glasgow and other really big British cities then so be it. Surely it is just a matter of time? In terms of gang culture, crack down hard, zero tolerance. But until you reform the woeful education system and legalize drugs then gang culture will continue to flourish. As the education system is unlikely to change and drugs will never be legalized, the Met and co best start taking delivery of firearms for all officers ASAP.

GH, drainage cleaner, male,
37, honours degree, privately educated

* Metropolitan Police Service unit set up to investigate and inform people about black gun crime, with special attention being placed on shootings relating to the illegal sale of drugs. The initiative was set up in March 1998 by black people following a series of shootings in the London boroughs of Lambeth and Brent.

I think that we could be doing more to tackle gang culture and I do think that instilling fear into these areas would help to control the issue. However, it is very risky to arm the police as very easily a situation of police vs gangs could develop, as it has in the USA. We need instead to take the burden of regulation and paperwork from the police force and allow them to more effectively police our streets. I also think that task forces could be developed to specifically tackle gang culture and gang war zones that have developed in our cities. Unfortunately a lot of this culture has developed from the way that our country has been run from the top. The options that a typical gang member has at the age of 10 are terrifying and it is the easy option for them to slip into a gang; thus what really is needed is political action to improve the prospects of young people in poorer areas and re-engage the next generation before they become disillusioned.

PS, city stockbroker,
34, male, privately educated

Gang culture is such an alien idea for me that I find it difficult to believe that groups can simply go around with blatant disrespect for human life. The whole idea has been beefed up through various TV shows and while I find it hard to believe that certain groups can be taken in by this, it has happened. I am convinced that arming all police is not the answer. What I do find hard to swallow is the fact that there exists 'no go areas' in certain suburbs and here, I think the police forces should go in and weed out the leaders and the vulnerable followers to protect them from themselves and their peers. Perhaps I believe in Utopia. But living in a country where the police are all armed, it doesn't stop the gang culture. Being armed with a taser is probably more of a deterrent than a firearm. A strange analysis? As a hooded individual causing trouble, I would probably be more worried about being on the receiving end of thousands of volts than waiting for an armed police officer to resort to the last resort and pulling out a gun. Or is that just me?

HS, British diplomatic community member,
45, male, lives in Belgium

These are not sensible alternatives. Gang culture grows for social reasons and these need tackling first. A happier society would not produce gangs. Just having more guns around only adds to future dangers. No one apart from some farmers needs a gun. Those who enjoy using guns in sports should only be able to do so in clubs. Until such a society exists the police may need, occasionally, to have a gun for defence of themselves and others. We are lucky not to live in the USA and must take great care not to become the same.

JC, retired religious education teacher,
69, female, public sector

Their secret views: your successful business

The views of these people are unedited; they are exactly how your employees, customers and shareholders feel. They are the mixture of our society that makes up life's rich and colourful tapestry.

The hardest part for me is to allow all these opinions in, without trying to change the path of some thoughts, or influence others – what has this taught me? Churchill was right: 'You cannot please all the people all the time'. But as I would say: 'In successful business, you need to give it a good try!'

The key to any successful business is not to make quick judgements built on only a few comments – we all differ so much in our views, but fundamentally we all have inner core beliefs which are similar. To be successful you need to understand all your customer base, you need to ensure your employees understand your customer base, and most of all you need to segment your customer base and talk to them accordingly. Why? Because we are all different, and businesses that acknowledge this and embrace it are businesses that thrive and achieve greatness.

Chapter Five
The world tomorrow
Embrace the future

Marketing in today's world

Sales and marketing will and should always go hand-in-hand; the most successful of businesses look to integrate their efforts to gain maximum results in a cluttered marketplace with savvy and constantly more demanding consumers. Businesses rely on word of mouth, personal recommendations, advocates of the product and a little luck to make a marketing plan work. When you are a large corporate company you can employ creative agencies that will either run your entire marketing team for you, or look to carry out specific campaigns, from concept of a single campaign to launch a new product or sell something established to a new audience. A creative team will scope the market, identify its target audience to establish the best results, develop an appropriate creative vision of artwork/design, choose the media and channel strategy accordingly, and then launch in a time-specific manner to gain maximum return on investment.

However, for an SME to gain 'best bang for its buck' it is a terrifyingly complex question of 'above or below the line' or now even 'push or pull' advertising and marketing. In short 'above' the line is all the media that shouts to anyone passing: TV, radio, posters, billboards, across-track adverts; whilst 'below' is slightly more targeted and measurable with promotional codes given to people who either buy specific magazines, newspapers or receive direct mail so you can control those who see your message a little better. Also sometimes known as 'push or pull' media, you 'push' TV or radio adverts onto people, but internet adverts are normally requested – so the consumer is 'pulling' up the website. Thus 'pull' media is allowing the consumer to drive the advert to them at a relevant moment in time.

So an SME could be excused for being afraid of what to test first. TV advertising is very expensive, not only the time slots to air the advert on the TV but the pure production of the advert. Radio is also costly and very hard to target the correct people, or to actually drive sales as opposed to just generate brand awareness. Magazine and newspaper print can be very expensive in some publications and results are often limited, or very reliant on that day's news or weather. Direct mail can be costly and time consuming; although very measurable you do need data, names and addresses of people to write to and a good message to communicate.

It is always best to wait until your business has been established a little while so that you understand which offerings bring you the best results before you dabble too much into marketing, as you can waste considerable time and money getting this wrong. Panic not – the world of social media has opened up opportunities to gain customer insight into what could work for your business. It can allow you to test offers, run a variety of campaigns and to really test your customer responses – then you use that knowledge to gain real traction with the more traditional advertising channels and routes to market.

With that in mind here are a few things you should know about the world in which we market our businesses:

- If you think you need to embrace social media, the smart phone, the app and all that is great with technology on the move, then you are correct. Ignore this market at your peril.

- I grew up and got my marketing qualifications long before Facebook, Twitter and smartphones existed. I do, however, bow to the power they hold – but I am not totally convinced they will do enough alone to launch and maintain a business. You hear of marketing campaigns going 'viral' which like any good disease analogy simply means it has spread uncontrollably and is now unstoppable.

- This is great in a world where you want to communicate with your customers, but if your brand has gone 'viral' in a less than positive manner then it is still uncontrollable and unstoppable! One recent marketing disaster saw YouTube footage of delivery men playing football with a new computer. The footage clearly depicted the sounds of the screen glass sloshing around as the item was 'kicked' up the drive. The uniform of the delivery driver was blazing out the name of the firm and as a result the company lost a considerable amount of their market share and are still trying to recover in the eyes of both customers and consumers.

- The voucher websites that offer discounts to people if they buy through them recently saw a small family business offer cupcakes at a half price rate for Valentine's Day – a really good idea to launch your online business and drum up some customers who should repeat purchase for future guaranteed revenues. However, the company never restricted the order number and got a magnificent response which resulted in 12,000 orders for time-critical delivery. They went bust.

Marketing now can be more dangerous than ever before. If you run a campaign you have to ensure you have engaged everyone involved, briefed your sales teams, brought your marketing team up to speed with price/product and potential future changes not only to the structure but to the entire process of any purchase. If you are going to offer a 'free gift', will it fit into the packaging already? You don't want to incur extra costs.

If you are offering money off, does this need a minimum order value? It is all simple straightforward thinking but in the heat of the moment you will be amazed how many people say 'let's just put it out there and see what happens!' In today's marketing world you might not get another chance. So test – test small, test frequently and test cautiously. If your advert does go viral you could be speaking to the world – just make sure you really have something worthwhile to say, and say something that you want them to hear!

Making money from technology

If you want to make money from technology, here are a few facts to help you:

- The average lifespan of computers in developed countries has dropped from six years in 1997 to just two years in 2005, and some believe it is even less now.

- Mobile phones have a lifecycle of less than two years in developed countries; it is believed the average was 18 months in 2010.

- 183 million computers were sold worldwide in 2004 – 11.6 per cent more than in 2003. In 2011 it was estimated that 10 computers were bought every second.

- According to Gartner Dataquest, in April 2002 the 1 billionth personal computer was shipped. The second billion mark was supposedly reached in 2007.

- How many computers are actually in use? Forrester Research reported that there were over 1 billion PCs in use worldwide by the end of 2008.

- With PC adoption in emerging markets growing fast, Forrester predicts that there will be more than 2 billion PCs in use by 2015. Therefore, whereas it took 27 years to reach the 1 billion mark, it will take only seven to grow from 1 billion to 2 billion.

- 674 million mobile phones were sold worldwide in 2004 – 30 per cent more than in 2003.
- 8 trillion text messages will be sent in 2012.
- There are 5.9 billion mobile subscribers (that's 87 per cent of the world population). Growth is led by China and India, which now account for over 30 per cent of world subs.
- Mobile devices sales rose in 2011, with smartphones showing strongest growth.
- There are now 1.2 billion mobile web users worldwide, based on the latest stats for active mobile-broadband subscriptions worldwide; Asia is top region.
- South Korea and Japan lead in mobile-broadband penetration with 91 and 88 per cent respectively.
- Mobile devices account for 8.49 per cent of global website hits.

We had more than 425 million mobile monthly active users in December 2011. In 2011, mobile usage of Facebook increased in markets around the world, including major developed markets such as the United States where smartphone penetration grew rapidly... improving our mobile products and increasing mobile usage of Facebook are key company priorities that we believe are critical to help us maintain and grow our user base and engagement over the long term. We expect consumers around the world will continue to increase the amount of time they spend and the information they share and consume through mobile devices.

Facebook IPO statement (February, 2012)

It is worth noting that:

- Many mobile web users are mobile-only, ie they do not, or very rarely, use a desktop, laptop or tablet to access the web. Even in the United States, 25 per cent of mobile web users are mobile-only.

- But consumers are also rapidly embracing mobile e-mail, IM (instant messaging) and MMS (multimedia messaging services).

- A2P (application-to-person SMS) – eg automated alerts from banks, offers from retailers, m-tickets – is expected to overtake person-to-person SMS in 2016.

The mobile phone market: the future and your business

How consumers use mobiles

What do consumers use their mobiles for?

Japanese consumers are still more advanced in their mobile behaviour, using mobile web, apps and e-mail more, but US and European users text and play more games. Most popular mobile destinations are news and information, weather reports, social networking, search and maps. US consumers prefer mobile browsers for banking, travel, shopping, local info, news, video, sports and blogs and prefer apps for games, social media, maps and music.

Surveys show that in all countries more consumers use their browser than apps and only a minority will use web or apps exclusively.

Mobile searches in particular have quadrupled in the last year, and for many items one in seven searches are now mobile. And 71 per cent of smartphone users that see TV, press or online ads do a mobile search. If they do that search, you need to ask yourself – will they find your mobile site or that of your competitors?

Mobile apps: do you need one?

Over 300,000 mobile apps have been developed in three years, and over that time apps have been downloaded 10.9 billion times. But demand for downloaded mobile apps is expected to peak in 2013. The most used mobile apps in the US are games, news, maps, social networking and music. Facebook, Google Maps and The Weather Channel (TWC) rule.

But does reality match the hype around apps? The average download price of a mobile app is falling rapidly on all vendor app stores, except Android. And one in four mobile apps once downloaded are never used again.

Mobile payments

Paying by mobile, ie m-payments, will be worth US$240 billion in 2011 and could be over US$1 trillion by 2015. Purchasing digital goods is the largest segment ahead of physical goods, near-field communications (NFC), m-banking and money transfer. The biggest market today is Japan, but in the future it could be China.

Japan sets the precedent for m-payments: 47 million Japanese have adopted tap-and-go phones, but the technology is expected to take off elsewhere as the world adopts NFC. In China alone, there will be 169 million users of tap-and-go payments in 2013.

M-commerce (shopping online) is predicted to reach US$119 billion in 2015, with Japan remaining king. Top m-commerce retailers globally include Taobao, Amazon and eBay. The US m-commerce market will be worth US$31 billion by 2016.

One in eight mobile subscribers will use m-ticketing in 2015 for airline, rail and bus travel, festivals, cinemas and sports events.

Mobile financial services (MFS) and m-banking

It is estimated that between 500 million and 1 billion people will access financial services by mobile by 2015. The MFS market will be dominated by Asia, driven by mobile operator-led initiatives in developing nations to bank the unbanked. Remittance/transfers by mobile are growing three times faster than m-banking.

> In the last 12 months, customers around the world have ordered more than US$1 billion of products from Amazon using a mobile device.
>
> Jeff Bezos, founder and CEO of Amazon.com (July 2010)

Mobile subscriptions

At the end of 2011, there were 5.9 billion mobile subscriptions, estimates The International Telecommunication Union (2011). That is equivalent to 87 per cent of the world's population – a huge increase from 5.4 billion in 2010 and 4.7 billion mobile subscriptions in 2009.

Mobile subscription in the developed world has reached saturation point with at least one cell phone subscription per person. This means market growth is being driven by demand from the developing world, led by rapid mobile adoption in China and India, the world's most populous nations. These two countries collectively added 300 million new mobile subscriptions in 2010 – that's more than the total number of mobile subscribers in the United States.

At the end of 2011 there were 4.5 billion mobile subscriptions in the developing world (76 per cent of global subscriptions). Mobile penetration in the developing world now is 79 per cent, with Africa being the lowest region worldwide at 53 per cent.

According to YouTube internal data, there are 200 million mobile video playbacks every day on YouTube.

We're also seeing a huge positive revenue impact from mobile, which has grown 2.5 times in the last 12 months to a run rate of over $2.5 billion.

Larry Page, CEO, Google

Let's turn to mobile advertising. Larry mentioned $2.5 billion as a run rate. Our revenue growth continues to accelerate even in mobile, driven primarily by mobile search... Many advertisers have greatly increased the size and frequency of their mobile campaigns. Mobile is becoming a must-have. This includes clients like InterContinental Hotels Group, which spans pretty much across our entire portfolio of properties, including mobile search, mobile GDN and AdMob.

Nikesh Arora, SVP, Google.
Q3 2011 Earnings Call October, 2011

Whether to have a mobile site or a mobile app and which to develop first depends on what kind of product you have. If most people are going to find you through search then you should optimize your site for mobile web, but if you think you have a big enough fan base and you can cut through the clutter of getting people to download your app, then you can have a more immersive experience by creating an app.

Chet Fenster, MEC Entertainment (November 2011)

With thanks for the support of and information from mobiThinking and Market Global (Global Mobile Statistics 2012).

Chapter Six
The world's gone crazy
A sign of the times!

I often read the papers in the morning and think 'that cannot possibly be true' – in a world where people have got so time-short, rushed and hurried, or just so plain lazy that they buy ready-grated cheese and cut-up lettuce to save time. By contrast, you have to fill your own car with petrol. I would like to say nothing ever surprises me – but then you read things like the following stories in the papers and you just think – REALLY, how can I run a business in this world!?

These are all true stories, all occurring in 2012, most within the first half of the year, so these things happen frequently. With thanks to those papers who published them, to those who made them possible, and to the excellent summary made available in *The Week* publication, to allow me to keep abreast of such occurrences, without missing any!

> *A town council has banned a pensioner from his allotment in case he breaks his hip and sues. Eastwood Council told Arthur Martin, 73, that they had a 'duty of care' to protect him, and gave him three weeks to vacate the allotment. 'If this guy's hip pops out again, as it has in the past, and he ends up in a wheelchair, what would people say?' said the council leader.*

*A town hall clock that had chimed every 15 minutes for
146 years was silenced in March 2012 after one local resident
complained about the noise. The owners of the building in
Farnham, Surrey, have turned the chimes off while they investigate
noise levels.*

*Research by Which? has found that the terms and conditions
on some shopping websites are longer than Shakespeare's longest
play. PayPal's small print runs to 36,275 words; Hamlet has a
mere 30,066.*

*As part of an initiative to cut red tape, the government has
published a 24-page document for a consultation into ice-cream
van noise. Among the proposals are an increase in the maximum
length of the chimes (from 4 seconds to 12) and an extension of
the permitted chiming hours to after 7 pm. The Department for
Environment, Food and Rural Affairs launched the consultation
as part of the government's Red Tape Challenge, a campaign to
'reduce unnecessary burdensome regulation on businesses'.*

*Forget baby showers; the latest trend to arrive from the
United States is the 'gender reveal party'. Mothers-to-be gather
their loved ones around, then cut into a cake. If the sponge is pink,
it's a girl; if it's blue, a boy. Some hosts are so keen to enjoy the
surprise themselves, they ask the hospital to send the sonogram
straight to the baker. In the United States, the nibbles are themed
according to the foods the mother has been craving, and guests
dress in either pink or blue to confirm their prediction.*

*Residents of six East London apartment blocks were told that
surface-to-air missile systems would be positioned on their
rooftops, to protect London from terrorist attacks during the
2012 Olympics. The rockets were manned 24-7, and remained in
place for two months.*

A sixth-form college in Essex has begun sending its A level students text messages containing 'top revision tips'. These include: 'work now and you'll reap the benefits later', 'you can work and play but you need the correct balance', and 'keep hydrated – it's key to success'. Pupils at Havering College say the messages are 'obvious', 'annoying' and 'distracting'.

The changing face of the Church of England was showcased at the 2012 International Christian Resources Exhibition, the trade fair for all things clerical. Among the products on display were clerical shirts with floral, paisley and leopard print patterns – aimed at women priests – and pulpit lecterns with iPad docks.

Public officials have been told to avoid using the word 'obese', as it could be considered 'derogatory'. Draft guidance issued by the National Institute for Health and Clinical Excellence (NICE) encourages councils and the NHS to focus on positive goals – such as achieving a 'healthier weight' – rather than obesity. The advice is from the quango's latest report, Obesity: Working with Local Communities.

A judge at Chelmsford Crown Court has advised jurors on how to cross the road from the main court building to the courtroom. 'I have to warn you for health and safety reasons to cross at the traffic lights,' said Christopher Ball QC. 'But you can make the decision to cross where you want.' In the end, the jurors were escorted by a court official.

The authorities in New York are cracking down on the use of potentially offensive words in school tests. Among 50 words and phrases banned by the city's Department of Education are: 'dinosaurs', which might offend creationists; 'birthdays' as Jehovah's Witnesses do not celebrate them; and 'homes with swimming pools' because not everyone has one.

Cockney rhyming slang is dying out and being replaced by newer slang terms such as OMG (Oh my God) says the Museum of London. The Museum's survey found that while just 20 per cent of Londoners had heard the phrase 'brown bread' (dead) in the last six months, 35 per cent had heard the word 'reem' (attractive) and 38 per cent had heard 'sick' used to mean 'good'.

A fire brigade that sent 25 fire fighters to help a stricken seagull in a shallow pond – and then told them not to enter the water – has defended its action as 'standard procedure'. The London Fire Brigade said it was normal for 25 men to attend a water rescue, and that the crews left Carshalton Ponds in South London because the gull 'wasn't in distress'. The bird, which was caught in a plastic bag, was saved by a local wildlife volunteer.

The Health and Safety Executive has set up a myth-busting panel to highlight councils and employers who over-zealously interpret its rules – forcing trapeze artists to wear hard hats, for example, or banning candy floss on sticks. However, they insisted that the case of the stricken gull (see above) wasn't 'about health and safety at all'.

Chapter Seven
The 100 Matrix
What people really think

So you think you know your market. You think you understand how your customers feel and what they want from the world today.

The purpose of this research was to see if people who had similar jobs had in fact similar views on society and life today. I carried out the research personally; it was done via a face-to-face questionnaire or an anonymous e-mail survey. No names were taken and the individuals asked were people I did not know personally. The techniques I used to find similar job roles, business titles or vocations varied in difficulty. For example, the taxi drivers were all parked up under London Bridge so I just went along with my clipboard. The professionals with exact job titles were identified by a variety of methods including listed data, social media and business premises and offices. I also visited playgrounds, the city, schools and government buildings – in all of which people were very helpful.

The questions were again all written with the help of the industry panel and all had to be answered with a 'yes', 'no' or 'indifferent' answer. No further comment was allowed as I wanted to establish a voting process, to force a final outcome.

What I wanted to understand from the results is: can you group people together by profession, age and beliefs to be able to gain better understanding of your customer base? After all, if you really knew who your customers were then you could target them with messages and products that worked for them. You could almost guarantee a response built on information prior to any form of marketing or communication.

Understanding your customer base is crucial to any business, not only to retain happy current customers but also to target new, similar customers to add to the retention pot. We must not forget your employees, team or staff – if they all feel the same way and it's not the same as the management or your customers feel, then that will need addressing quickly before the lack of harmony starts affecting the bottom line.

The results from these views will enable the reader to build a picture that is relevant to their customers, their industry or sector. It will establish how their business can be improved as a result. On the flip side it will demonstrate how potential or existing customers REALLY feel about life and the business world around them.

The questions

10 questions asked to 10 groups of 10 people

1 Should our police be armed?

2 Should companies have to contribute towards their employees' pensions?

3 Should any company be forced to employ a certain percentage of people, dependent on gender, age, religion or ethnic background?

4 Has health and safety gone too far in the workplace and society?

5 Do you feel proud of the British business economy?

6 Should people pay for their university education?

7 Should we bring UK borrowing down and reduce our debt?

8 Do we pay too much tax?

9 Should doctors, dentists and healthcare be free to all?

10 Should UK borders be closed?

The answers

FIGURE 7.1   Stockbrokers

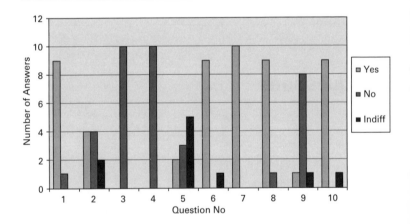

FIGURE 7.2   City bankers

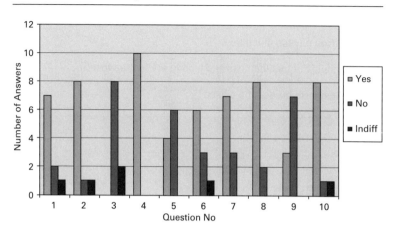

FIGURE 7.3   Heads of FTSE companies

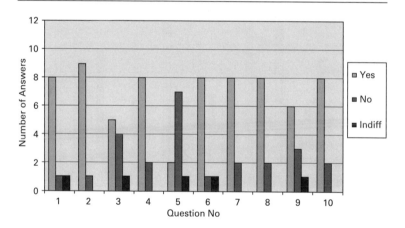

FIGURE 7.4   London taxi drivers

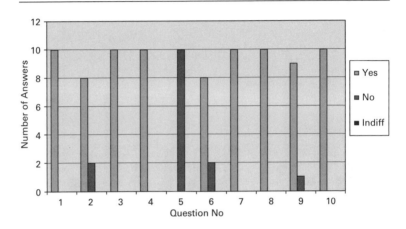

FIGURE 7.5   Key account directors

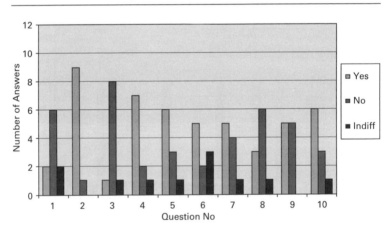

FIGURE 7.6   SME account directors

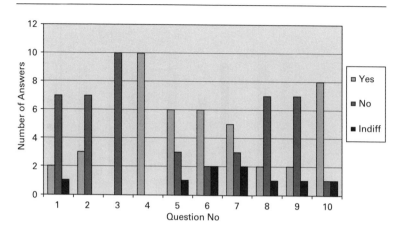

FIGURE 7.7   CEOs

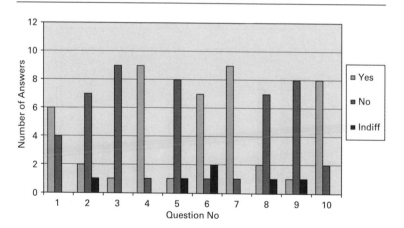

FIGURE 7.8 Stay-home mothers

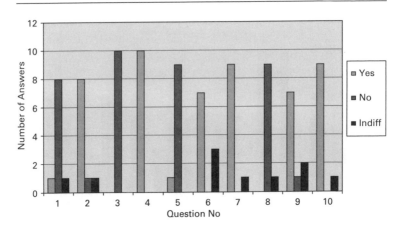

FIGURE 7.9 Working parents

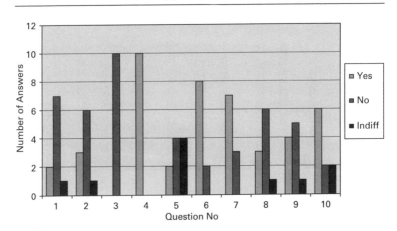

FIGURE 7.10   Civil servants

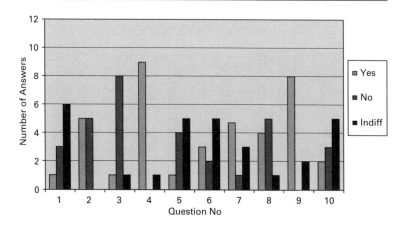

FIGURE 7.11 Summary of responses

	Question 1			Question 2			Question 3			Question 4			Question 5			Question 6			Question 7			Question 8			Question 9			Question 10			Average		
	Yes	No	Indiff	Yes	No	Indiff	Yes	No	Indiff	Yes	No	Indiff	Yes	No	Indiff	Yes	No	Indiff	Yes	No	Indiff	Yes	No	Indiff	Yes	No	Indiff	Yes	No	Indiff	Yes	No	Indiff
Stockbrokers	9	1	0	4	4	2	0	10	0	10	0	0	2	3	5	9	0	1	10	0	0	9	1	0	1	8	1	9	0	1	6.3	2.7	1
City bankers	7	2	1	8	1	1	0	8	2	10	0	0	4	6	0	6	3	1	7	3	0	8	2	0	3	7	0	8	1	1	6.1	3.3	0.6
Heads of FTSE companies	8	1	1	9	1	0	5	4	1	8	2	0	2	7	1	8	1	1	8	2	0	8	2	0	6	3	1	8	2	0	7	2.5	0.5
London taxi drivers	10	0	0	8	2	0	0	10	0	10	0	0	0	10	0	8	2	0	10	0	0	10	0	0	9	1	0	10	0	0	7.5	2.5	0
Key account directors	2	6	2	9	1	0	1	8	1	7	2	1	6	3	1	5	2	3	6	4	0	3	6	1	7	3	0	3	5	2	4.9	4	1.1
SME account directors	2	7	1	3	7	0	0	10	0	10	0	0	6	3	1	6	2	2	5	4	1	2	7	1	2	7	1	8	0	2	4.4	4.7	0.9
CEOs	6	4	0	2	7	1	1	9	0	9	1	0	1	8	1	7	1	2	9	0	1	2	7	1	2	8	0	7	3	0	4.6	4.8	0.6
Stay-home mothers	1	8	1	8	1	1	0	10	0	10	0	0	1	9	0	7	0	3	8	1	1	0	9	1	8	0	2	9	0	1	5.2	3.8	1
Working parents	2	7	1	3	6	1	0	10	0	10	0	0	2	4	4	8	2	0	7	3	0	3	6	1	6	4	0	4	3	3	4.5	4.5	1
Civil servants	1	3	6	5	5	0	1	8	1	9	0	1	1	4	5	3	2	5	6	0	4	4	5	1	2	4	4	8	0	2	4	3.1	2.9
Total	48	39	13	59	35	6	8	87	5	93	5	2	25	57	18	67	15	18	76	17	7	49	45	6	46	45	9	74	14	12	54.5	35.9	9.6

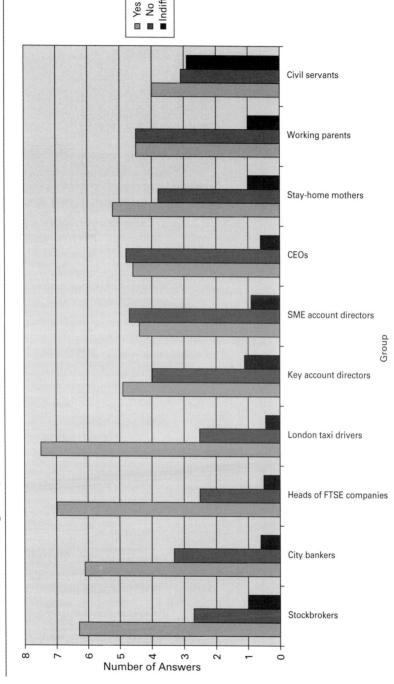

FIGURE 7.12 Average responses – answer comparison

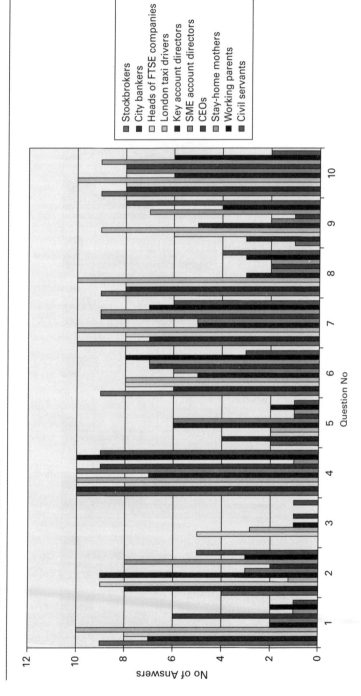

FIGURE 7.13 All 'Yes' answers

FIGURE 7.14 All 'No' answers

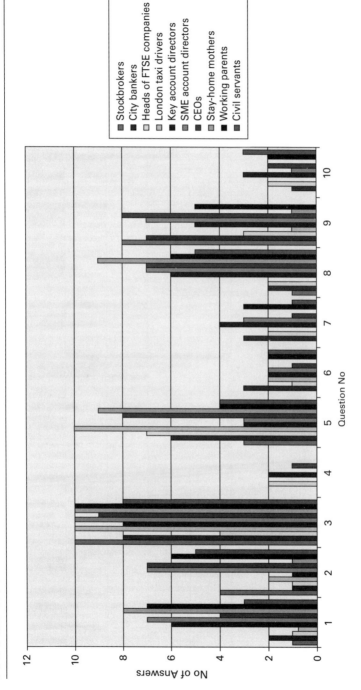

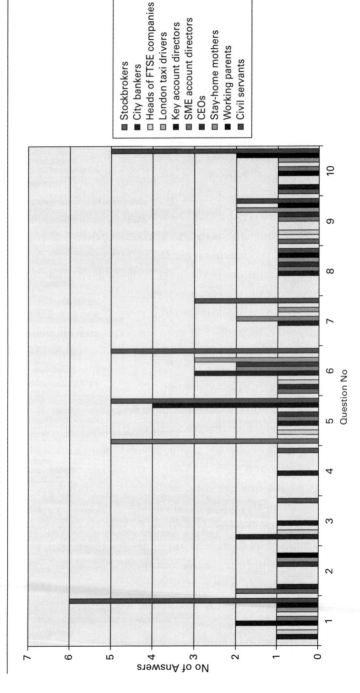

FIGURE 7.15 All 'Indifferent' answers

The results

As a business owner it is vitally important to remember that ultimately everyone is different, you will not be able to, and nor should you, have a 'one-size-fits-all' solution for all of your customers.

The cleverer you can make your customer relationship management (CRM) system the more intelligence you can gather about your customers, which in turn will help you market to them to enable up-selling and cross-selling of your products or business offering. This research delivered surprising results in some areas, but overall it clearly demonstrated that people in the same job roles predominantly have the same beliefs and behavioural tendencies. They feel the same about the environment they live and work in.

So why is this relevant? It allows you to appreciate the importance of segmentation. If you have the intelligence and information about your customers, albeit in the simplest form of gender, age or job title, it will allow you to better sell and market to them. The tone you take with your customers in marketing communications can be cleverly tailored to allow you to push the buttons that turn that group of individuals on. When you carry out the Dice Matrix Model you will, by the nature of the business model, gather information about your customers. When you do the customer survey element there is nothing to stop you asking a few basic questions about age group, profession and the like to help you to identify and segment your current customers.

Just imagine holding the insight and the knowledge of who your customers are, understanding who buys from you and why they buy: it would allow you to go to any data-house and purchase profiled lists of names and addresses that match your customers. You could then carry out a direct, targeted marketing campaign at people who match the profile and segmentation of your business database. Knowing the most you can about your customers and their behaviours can only bring brilliance to your sales and marketing campaigns which in turn is the heart, and life blood, of any growing business.

Big corporations don't invest millions into loyalty cards and schemes purely to keep us loyal; they are a tool to help businesses gather enormous amounts of data and intelligence on individuals, My local supermarket loyalty card tells the owners what I buy, the time of day I buy it, and that I have children, but what they can actually deduce from my shopping habits informs them of so much more about me. They can conclude I am not a vegetarian, and I love fish, I like to drink all types of wine, my husband likes beer; they know our children's ages due to the clothes and types of food, my dress size, what films and music I like, my favourite chocolate bar, that I work full-time and grab sandwiches from their stores all over the UK at random times, that I stay away from home a lot and eat breakfast in their cafés for quick meetings. They could understand and manipulate me to do almost anything with the information they hold about me. Add that to my iPhone telling the Maps application where I am at any given moment, and then take the data that inevitably Sky TV holds about what I watch and what I record on my digital box and I am totally understood by three organizations. Does it worry me? No. Do I feel a bit weird and uncomfortable when I get my voucher offers through the mail from said supermarket and they are so targeted towards me it makes me feel a bit uncomfortable that they know I would like money off Nivea facecream and soft fresh baked cookies? Yes. But what I do believe is that marketing will only get better. Poorly targeted marketing and sales campaigns will be a thing of the past – I will only have to talk to companies I want to buy from because nothing else will get through to me, or be communicated to me.

The times ahead are very exciting; the world five years ago was such a different place, now we know, see and have so much more at our fingertips than ever before. We are more demanding than ever as consumers. Should you and your business carry out market research like this on your customer database? Yes. Why? Because all your competitors will be.

Chapter Eight
The Dice Matrix Model
Time to succeed

We all get customer feedback, we all get employee feedback, no matter how big or how small we are as a business. This provides essential input into our future state as an organization.

They say all the best solutions are simple ones and this model is no exception. But by using the Dice Matrix Model (DMM), you will get some astounding outputs that allow you to build up your business on stronger foundations to dizzy heights. The DMM is made even easier by a simple digital application into which you input your results and from which it calculates your outputs. The easy-to-use app will deliver results that enable you to identify your business risks and opportunities.

You can compare your customers' perceptions with those of your employees with 36 unique questions: six sets of six questions that deliver insight into your business. By posing these cleverly designed sets of DMM questions to your customers and then, with slight variations, to your employees, you will have a greater capacity to understand your strengths and weaknesses better than any SWOT (Strengths, Weaknesses, Opportunities, Threats) or any PEST (Political, Economic, Strategic, Tactical) analysis would provide. DMM provides input from every touch-point of your business and from every perception, angle and varied opinion, which in turn allows you to carry out detailed gap analysis to identify your opportunities and risks.

The Dice Matrix Model will also allow you to calibrate when you and your employees think you are doing well, but your customers are left wanting. DMM will allow you to analyse real-time feedback about your business and identify the real 'voice of the customer' so when, and if, your employees tell you things are working but your customers are not convinced, you can identify the real issues and address the real needs of your business.

If your employees hate doing a specific task and it turns out your customers don't rate that part of your business, you can and should address this to get happier, more motivated employees, achieving a better return on investment and improved outputs from your retained employee base.

DMM will work for any business; from the one-man-band (so long as you are honest with your input!) to a large multinational corporation, this simple model works and allows strategic gap analysis like never before. If you carry out the Dice Matrix Model at least once a year, or after any major change, growth, or merger occurs within your business then this will enable you to look at what really needs to be done. It will give you the chance to cut through the political and external noise in any business and drill straight down to the issues that affect your business and your unique selling points.

How DMM works

Figure 8.1 provides a simple illustration of the model, which consists of three stages and levels of outputs:

1 tactical questions for customers and employees (first outputs);

2 strategic alignment of tactical results (second outputs);

3 gap analysis (third outputs).

The answers are overlaid to turn the outputs into a 3D matrix to enable you to pull your responses from tactical answers into a strategic plan to drive your business forward.

The outputs will also allow you to get cross-referencing from inside your business to external brand perceptions. Then you can take your outputs and compare them against the leading businesses and their average means scores, or against customer survey/satisfaction results to see who you currently stack up against and what you need to do to rival your competitors more closely.

FIGURE 8.1 The Dice Matrix Model: stages

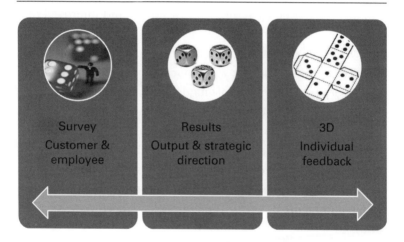

To download the DMM Application or for more information and insight on the research please visit **www.dicematrixconsulting.com**.

However, if you don't want to rely on a machine, or you work in an environment that means your employees and customers don't have access to a computer or deal with you via the internet, you can still make the DMM work for you. I have carried out the matrix with various companies, all of whom have found it very useful. Through this chapter you will be able to see how you could do this with a good old-fashioned pen and paper, so whichever works better for your employees, staff or customers means you can get the answers you need – now!

Stage 1: tactical questions for customers and employees (first outputs)

There are six sides to each dice, each representing an aspect of your business on which you want feedback:

1 The Customer

2 The Sale

3 The Product

4 The Service

5 The Aftercare

6 The People

and six questions to each side, giving 36 questions and answers for each group (customers and employees). The questions are listed in Table 8.1, and the model brought to life with a detailed example in Figure 8.2.

TABLE 8.1 Dice Matrix Model: tactical questions for customers and employees (first outputs)

	Ques No	Customers' questions	Employees' questions
Customer	1	Did we treat you well?	Do we treat our customers well?
	2	Would you use us again?	If you needed one of our products or services would you buy from us?
	3	Would you recommend us?	Would you recommend us to your friends and family?
	4	Have you recommended us?	Have you recommended us or used us?
	5	Would you consider working for us?	Would you consider suggesting to a friend that they should work for us?
	6	Did we exceed your expectations?	Did you believe we exceeded our customers' expectations?
Sales	1	Was the price right?	Do we charge the right price?
	2	Was the selection and range correct?	Do you feel we offer and sell the correct selection and range?
	3	Was the appearance and packaging satisfactory?	Do you feel our packaging is satisfactory and the overall appearance of our product is good?
	4	Did you enjoy the purchasing experience?	Do you think we do the most we can to ensure the customer's purchasing experience is enjoyable?
	5	Would you buy again?	Would you buy from us from one of our competitors?
	6	Were you pleased with your purchase?	If you bought from us do you think you would be pleased with your purchase?

TABLE 8.1 *continued*

	Ques No	Customers' questions	Employees' questions
Product	1	Was the quality good?	Do you feel we offer good quality?
	2	Was the delivery/execution carried out to schedule?	Do we deliver to our customers on schedule?
	3	Did we meet expectations?	Do you think we meet our customers' expectations?
	4	Did you return anything?	Do you think we get too many returns?
	5	Did you feel you got value for money?	Do you believe we offer overall value for money?
	6	Do you like the company brand?	Do you like the company brand?
Service	1	Could you find us easily?	Do you think our advertising is effective?
	2	Was our web presence good?	Is our web presence good for our customers and for our internal intranet communications?
	3	Did we respond quickly to you?	Do we respond to our customers quickly?
	4	Did we communicate effectively?	Do we communicate effectively to you as an employee?
	5	Did we meet your needs?	Did we meet the needs of our customer base?
	6	Did you like us and our values?	Did you like the business brand and its values?

Aftercare	1	Did you feel embraced and valued?	Do we make our customers feel embraced and valued?
	2	Did we contact you again?	Do we contact our customers enough?
	3	Did you join our newsletter/ membership?	Do you think we offer our customers enough value from the newsletter/ membership?
	4	Did we welcome you as a customer?	Do we always welcome our customers and thank them for their business?
	5	Did we confirm your purchase, delivery and update you?	Do we do enough around the confirmation of the purchase, delivery and updates?
	6	Did we make you want to buy again from us?	Do you think most of our customers buy from us again?
People	1	Were we polite?	Are we polite to our customers and our colleagues?
	2	Did we match our brand promise?	Do we match our brand promise internally?
	3	Did we thank you?	Do we thank you enough for working so hard?
	4	Would you feel proud if you worked for us?	Do you feel proud to be part of this company and to work for us?
	5	Would you say we knew our business?	Would you say we knew our business?
	6	Did we answer all your queries and advise you well?	Do we answer all your queries and advise you well with your career and personal growth?

FIGURE 8.2 The Dice Matrix Model: questions

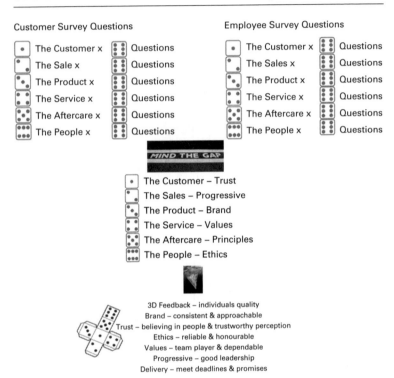

Customer questions will deliver 36 qualitative results multiplied by the number of customers from whom you received data – this gives you the first output of your DMM.

Employee questions will deliver 36 qualitative results multiplied by the number of employees who completed the survey – this gives you the second set of figures for your first output of your DMM.

Once you have downloaded the DMM application matrix, or have your pen and paper at hand if you prefer, you will be able to input the answers to the questions and then the system will generate tables and graphs to allow you to easily identify areas that your business and your customers agree on. These will either be great strengths where everyone is pulling together to create the perfect level of satisfaction and delivery of brand promise, or they will be areas where both parties agree they are doing badly, which will highlight quickly and effectively the areas that as a business you must address as a matter of urgency. These weaknesses, although they may appear very detrimental to your business initially, are actually very easily resolved as everyone considers they need improvement. You could turn these into win-wins across the organization. Your employees think there is room for improvement, so if you address these issues you can play back into the business that you listened to your employees and dealt with their concerns.

You will also please your customer base, as you can advertise that feedback given via consumer opinions has been taken up. As a business you listened to what was required and carried out improvements to directly affect the experience of your customer base, saying you genuinely listened to customer feedback and have, as a result, changed the way you do business to ensure a better level of service moving forwards.

Therefore, you will have the support of your customers as they would like to see improvements; you will also have the support of your employees as they have highlighted areas in need of improvement which will allow you to take them on the journey to address their concerns. You can use this output in marketing promotions, adverts, the opening to any additional surveys – to tell your customers about the 'new improved' service you now offer and in internal communications to tell your team/employees that you are listening and responding to what they tell you.

Stage 2: strategic alignment of tactical results (second outputs)

So you have completed your two surveys and you are looking at the results – what do they tell you? Well, not so fast, there is another dimension to the model which is vital in turning your results into tangible actions with deliverable goals. Once you have completed the DMM first stage you need to roll up the results to turn them from tactical to strategic outputs.

The six groups of attributes to which the questions are aligned will give you the overlay to bring your tactical answers to a strategic board debate, make decisions and bring your company to life.

Each group of questions aligns to a strategic element of your business: thus 'Customer' questions marry at the strategic level with 'Trust', and with a series of attributes this represents.

The old adage that the customer is always right kicks in here. As your customers are what deliver your turnover, you need to remember 'the customer is king'. So before you get into the tactical depths of your gap analysis you must first identify what needs addressing. This should not detract from the importance of the gap analysis but act as a guide to allow you to address issues with some direction. As tempting as it may be to dive right into the detail and get into 'solution mode', you must approach your detailed gap analysis with a focused, forensic approach that is driven by your survey responders not by your views of the output. So take all your customers' answers from the six questions in each segment, and roll them up into one percentage, combining the first two sections and the last two sections to give you real focus. Whichever overall areas from the six cube matrix get the best/worst scores, you will be able to strategize with confidence that the first part of the gap analysis you address will drive the best results, be the quickest to please your customer base and ensure that the DMM works effectively. Then you can work through the other issues in line with your new overarching, fact-based strategy to ensure you build the best foundations for your business to thrive and show real time results from the views of those who count.

TABLE 8.2 Example of strategic alignment to get tactical results

Who	Customer Matrix (in %s)	Sales Matrix (in %s)	Product Matrix (in %s)	Service Matrix (in %s)	Aftercare Matrix (in %s)	People Matrix (in %s)
Customer Answers	Q. 1	Q. 1	Q. 1	Q. 1	Q. 1	Q. 1
	Q. 2	Q. 2	Q. 2	Q. 2	Q. 2	Q. 2
	Q. 3	Q. 3	Q. 3	Q. 3	Q. 3	Q. 3
	Q. 4	Q. 4	Q. 4	Q. 4	Q. 4	Q. 4
	Q. 5	Q. 5	Q. 5	Q. 5	Q. 5	Q. 5
	Q. 6	Q. 6	Q. 6	Q. 6	Q. 6	Q. 6
Employee Answers	Q. 1	Q. 1	Q. 1	Q. 1	Q. 1	Q. 1
	Q. 2	Q. 2	Q. 2	Q. 2	Q. 2	Q. 2
	Q. 3	Q. 3	Q. 3	Q. 3	Q. 3	Q. 3
	Q. 4	Q. 4	Q. 4	Q. 4	Q. 4	Q. 4
	Q. 5	Q. 5	Q. 5	Q. 5	Q. 5	Q. 5
	Q. 6	Q. 6	Q. 6	Q. 6	Q. 6	Q. 6

TABLE 8.3 Answers to the customer element of the Matrix in detail

	Strongly Agree	Agree	Indifferent	Disagree	Strongly Disagree
Customer Q 1	23%	45%	10%	22%	0%
Customer Q 2	12%	72%	13%	1%	2%
Customer Q 3	13%	51%	35%	1%	0%
Customer Q 4	3%	9%	43%	42%	3%
Customer Q 5	0%	17%	17%	53%	13%
Customer Q 6	7%	23%	69%	1%	0%
TOTAL	58%	217%	187%	120%	18%

Combine segments 'Strongly agree' and 'Agree' and 'Disagree' and 'Strongly Disagree' to give you real strategic focus.

FIGURE 8.3 Summary of customer element of the Matrix – customer responses only

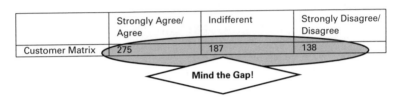

	Strongly Agree/ Agree	Indifferent	Strongly Disagree/ Disagree
Customer Matrix	275	187	138

Mind the Gap!

These figures would then be carried forward to the first line of the DMM strategic alignment of tactical output (second output) in Table 8.4 and repeated for all the other five sides of the Matrix using the customer survey responses.

The process could again be repeated for the employee's responses; although this is not essential at this stage, it may reveal some very good indications on future strategy.

Each strategy in turn is aligned with clear descriptive summaries to allow you to identify the issues and the areas of concern. So no matter how big or how small your business is, you will truly understand what needs addressing, how you can grow and improve your business and what the genuine real-time perception is of your business.

Take your outputs from both surveys and input the data into the DMM application. The application will work out your areas of concern and then from those questions, which are carefully designed to fit specific categories, you can identify which business strategies you need to address to deal with your gaps. You will then be able to tackle and concentrate on the sweet spots or the holes you have in your dealings with the customer, sale, product, service, aftercare or your people at a very high level – resulting in addressing everyone's issues at the genuine root cause.

Once you collate your results from both surveys you will establish areas of inconsistency: sometimes your customers will

TABLE 8.4   Dice Matrix Model: strategic alignment of tactical output (second outputs)

Tactical to Strategic alignment	Description	Strongly Agree/ Agree	Indifferent	Disagree/ Strongly Disagree
The Customer – Trust	Confidence, reliance, conviction, dependence	275	187	138
The Sale – Progressive	Growth, evolution, improvement, advancement			
The Product – Brand	Philosophy, trademarks, logo, image, make, product			
The Service – Values	Standards, ideas, concept			
The Aftercare – Principles	Ideology, dogma, credo, credibility			
The People – Ethics	Beliefs, codes, attitudinal data			

believe you are better than your employees do or vice versa. These are potentially high-risk or high-opportunity areas which will need addressing, but first you must analyse these differences and establish your official 'gap analysis'.

Stage 3: gap analysis (third outputs)

The outputs you get from the DMM that will need special attention are those that show gaps. Gap analysis is crucial to ensure you deliver the required action and address these issues – but when your customers and employees don't agree special care must be taken!

If your employees don't think they are rude, discourteous or obstructive to the sales process but all your customer survey insight tells you differently, you will need special training plans and schedules put in place to address these issues without demotivating and unsettling your employees. Unless of course the feedback is so severe you may wish to change them altogether!

I have used the DMM on many companies, some with hundreds of employees and huge turnovers and balance sheets and some with small budgets and limited customer insight. It makes no difference. Table 8.5 shows the results of DMM carried out by a small company, employing 23 people and turning over a modest amount. They had the desire to grow, but they wanted to ensure they had got the basics right first before they potentially took their eye off the ball from the day-to-day business to spend time creating a new channel and revenue stream.

They asked all their employees to complete the questionnaire online; it was anonymous to ensure they got good, honest and prompt response. They got 95 per cent take-up and most employees commented in the free text box that they were 'pleased and enthused' that they had been asked for their opinions, and had been given the opportunity to engage and apply input into the future of the business they worked for. The survey was kept simple with five response options, from strongly agree to strongly disagree.

The company also invited 2,500 customers to respond; all had bought before or were in the purchase process. The company did offer a small prize for completing the questionnaire, the winner to be picked at random by the closing day; this enabled them to get quick, timely responses and they also used it to capture data and cleanse their database. They had a response rate of 69 per cent which is very good for customer engagement. The survey output allowed them enough insight to get a really good understanding of what their customers and employees really thought.

TABLE 8.5 Dice Matrix Model: gap analysis results example (third outputs)

The 'Customer' Dice Matrix	Strongly Agree	Agree	Indifferent	Disagree	Strongly Disagree
1. Did we treat you well?	23%	**45%**	10%	22%	0%
Do we treat our customers well?	33%	**45%**	22%	0%	0%
OUTCOME	RO	**O**	R	HR	NA
2. Would you use us again?	12%	**72%**	13%	1%	2%
If you needed one of our products or services would you buy from us?	35%	**63%**	2%	0%	0%
OUTCOME	RO	**O**	O	R	R
3. Would you recommend us?	13%	**51%**	35%	1%	0%
Would you recommend us to your friends & family?	25%	23%	**40%**	12%	0%
OUTCOME	O	**RO**	R	HR	NA

TABLE 8.5   *continued*

The 'Customer' Dice Matrix	Strongly Agree	Agree	Indifferent	Disagree	Strongly Disagree
4. Have you recommended us?	3%	9%	**43%**	42%	3%
Have you recommended us or used us?	17%	**53%**	13%	17%	0%
OUTCOME	O	**O**	**HR**	HR	R
5. Would you consider working for us?	0%	17%	17%	**53%**	13%
Would you consider suggesting to a friend that they should work for us?	0%	10%	**55%**	12%	23%
OUTCOME	HR	R	**HR**	**HR**	HR
6. Did we exceed your expectations?	7%	23%	**69%**	1%	0%
Did you believe we exceed our customers' expectations?	**78%**	5%	16%	0%	1%
OUTCOME	**HR**	RO	**HR**	NA	NA
OUTPUT ANALYSIS	RO, RO, O, O, HR, HR	O, O, RO, O, R, RO	R, O, R, HR, HR, HR	HR, R, HR HR, HR, NA	NA, R, NA, R, HR, NA

Key: R = Risk
        HR = High Risk
        O = Opportunity
        RO = Risk with Opportunity   ☐ = Customer Response
        NA = No Action Required   ☐ = Employee Response

Table 8.5 describes what transpired from the two surveys with both the employees and the customers, and clearly shows gaps in perceptions between the two groups. The table depicts the output that came from the side of the 'Customer' DMM. So, if you look at the tactical to strategic alignment table (Table 8.4) you will see that the 'Customer' relates to the confidence, reliance, conviction and dependence they have with you, your employees and your business.

The example in Table 8.5 shows they do not need to address their overall customer service or offering, they need to simply maintain the good work they are doing. However in the third question they have generated a 'risk' output as their own employees would not recommend them to their friends or family, yet most customers would. This is a huge risk, but with the correct leverages and applications, training, and strategy put in place this could turn into an extra revenue stream, a chance for better quality of service, driving up the overall customer satisfaction, employee engagement and profitable business output.

This table is one of the six you would create to be able to address your business moving forward in all the areas of importance within your business.

Now the outputs have been plotted, identifying your risk areas, growth areas, high risk and high opportunity sectors, you need to work out and gain insight into how to deal with the outcome, how to process the information and what the definitions of risk, opportunity and high risk are in great detail. Once you get your gap analysis, however, you must not react quickly to those by 'sticking an Elastoplast' over the issues. You must take these tactical answers and address them by addressing your overarching business strategy. That way you will be able to address all of the customer issues from a higher level, not just address a few customer or employee issues without maximizing profitability.

Out of this DMM you will understand what is important to your customers, what is crucial to address in the short, medium and long term to help you build strategy and plan to be more profitable in the future. It will shine a light on any areas of the business that require changing and shaping to keep up with customer or employee demand. It will also act as a great input into your training and staff skills improvement planning, whether for new skills or just an up-skilling plan for the months/years ahead.

If you do nothing else to support your business growth and success this year – DO this Dice Matrix Model. Find time to test this tactical tool which will give you all the answers you need to make your business exponentially improve and flourish at a strategic level.

One stage further: the 3D dimension

If you wish to continue then it's all about your people, so to put it bluntly – 'Let's get your SHIT together', where SHIT = Sincerity, Honesty, Integrity, Trust.

If you want to take this model into a 3D dimension you can add a level of personal output. People buy people; it is why the art of selling is so important and always worth investing in. This section of the model is subjective as it can sway and skew the results by adding a personal opinion element to your business. However, if you are a large multinational, your people will be motivated by their manager far more than by corporate strategy. This 3D element will expose the members of the management team who are not motivating their people and leading the team with good leadership skills at the same time as highlighting those managers who take their people with them, no matter how hard the journey may be.

Build the third dimension by posing the questions to the business board or to individual employees in the leadership/management team. The business or individual 3D matrix can be completed by everyone on the company: board, shareholders,

TABLE 8.6   Dice Matrix Model: individual feedback intangible matrix

Intangible Quality	Strongly Agree/Agree	Indifferent	Disagree/ Strongly Disagree
Brand – consistent/ approachable			
Trust – believing in people/ trustworthy perception			
Ethics – reliable/ honourable			
Values – team player/ dependable			
Progressive – good leadership			
Delivery – meet deadlines/promises			

owners or a management team. Questions can be answered from either a corporate view or from a team's view of an individual. Both are very valuable, as from an individual's perspective this can allow 360-degree feedback in real time to address growth areas.

Depending on how big your organization is, remember that potentially when people are responding to this element they won't be able to distance themselves from the leadership team/ private company owner enough to be objective about the business brand and business versus individual trust. I would recommend setting this as a 'wearing your customer hat' exercise: 'if you were a customer would you like our brand, would you trust us, would you think we are ethical? Do you like our values, are we progressive as a company and do we deliver what we promise?' As a result of this positioning you should get a good understanding of the perception of these intangible assets (see Table 8.6).

The 3D dimension will allow you to see in forensic detail where you have great employee responses across many teams but where your gap analysis has identified one team as not being positive. This element of the matrix will help you ascertain if the team's unrest is due to the leadership skills of an individual rather than the overall company ethos itself. On a more positive note, it will help you to see if your management and leadership teams are the reason for such great results and will allow you to recognize your pockets of great achievement, to benchmark the rest of the company against these and share best practice from those positive responses.

Example questions for the brand matrix segment for an individual include:

1 Is your line manager consistent with their approach?

2 Does your manager treat the team respectfully?

3 Do you feel supported by your manager?

4 Do you think your manager deals with inefficiency correctly?

5 Do you receive enough coaching and encouragement?

6 Are your views listened to?

For more examples of each matrix side visit the website **www. dicematrixconsulting.com**.

Is it worth the effort? This 3D element of the DMM is always worth repeating with the management team/board/shareholders/stakeholders – individuals will gain 360-degree feedback on their management style and a consistent approach to what and who they believe they are. It will also allow businesses to gain insights to identify those with great potential and the young yet incredibly important rising stars in your organization. In turn this can help with succession planning and with an individual's development plans – and sometimes even reward and remuneration!

Chapter Nine
This way to success...

We have all attended training courses, got business books on our shelves that we have 'meant to read' or proposed to action – but I urge you to try this matrix model.

It is so easy and it will really enable you, like no other system, to get under the skin of your business and its issues.

Once you have completed the matrix for the first time you will make it part of your business's quarterly review; it will form part of your stake- and shareholder content for reviews.

This matrix model will allow you to clearly define the areas of your business you need to address and which ones you need to deal with quickly.

As they say, procrastination is the thief of all time... so go on, what are you waiting for?

To finish with one of my favourite quotes from one of my favourite, original, try-hard entrepreneurs:

This time next year... we'll be millionaires!

Index

NB: page numbers in *italic* indicate figures or tables

100 matrix
importance of 197–98
overview 184–85
questions 185–86
responses *186–96*

AdMob 179
Advertiser, The 62
ageing population, of UK 6–7
'AIDA' technique 19–20
Allen, Fred 58
Amazon 177, 178
American Express 15
Android 177
Apple 15, 19, 33, 41, 141–44, 198
Apprentice Scheme 42
Aquascutum 34
Aristotle 59, 61
Arora, Nikesh 179
Asia Society 40
Atkinson, Brooks 62
Australian, The 60

Ball, Christopher 182
Balls, Ed 113
Bank of England 13
Basel Convention on the Control of
        Transboundary Movements of
        Hazardous Wastes and their
        Disposal 40–41
BBC 35, 45
Believe in Gloucester 52
Bell, Alexander Graham 151
Berra, Yogi 58
Beveridge, William 111
Bezos, Jeff 178
Bismarck, Otto von 81
Blair, Tony 18, 114, 164
Boyle, Frankie 156
BP 81, 129

Bradford City FC 106
Brilliant, Ashleigh 62
British Airways 19
British American Tobacco 124
British Future 33
British Telecom 83
Brown, Gordon 18, 113, 130, 144,
        147
Brunel, Isambard Kingdom 118
Bruno, Giordano 58
Buffalo News 59, 61, 62
Buffett, Warren 62
Burke, Edmund 58
Burns, George 64
Bush, George W 127, 130
business landscape
current 12–14
post-war 10–12

Cameron, David 18, 107
Care Quality Commission 37
Carnegie, Andrew 58
China
emergence of 5
marketing, power of 48–49
Churchill, Winston 15, 64, 65, 170
City AM 52
Clarkson, Jeremy 155, 156
Cockerell, Christopher 118
ComRes 45, 54
Convention on Tobacco Control 48
Cook, Robin 80
Cooper Clarke, John 58
Crocs 34
customer satisfaction, importance of
        14–15

Daewoo 118
Daily Mail, The 27, 37
    Mail on Sunday, The 18

Daily Telegraph, The 17, 26, 29, 51, 52
Sunday Telegraph, The 22, 29, 33
Dales Farm 88
Darwin, Charles 58
Dell 41
Department of Health 44
Dice Matrix Model (DMM) 15, 111, 199–218
  3D dimension 216–18
    individual feedback matrix *217*
    value of 218
  business size 3, 200
  origins of 3
  purposes of 3–4, 199–200
  stage 1 202–07
    example *206*
    outputs 206–07
    questions *203–05*
  stage 2 208–10
    attributes and strategy 208, *209*
    collating results 210
  stage 3 212–16
    example gap analysis *213–14*
    strategy, importance of addressing 215
Dickens, Charles 60
Disraeli, Benjamin 60
Doctors.net.uk 53
Dyson 121–22
  Dyson, James 118

eBay 177
Employee Outlook Study 17
Energy Performance Certificates (EPCs) 12, 97

Facebook 172, 175, 177
Fairtrade and Rainforest Alliance 84
family businesses 4
Farrell, J G 63
Fenster, Chet 179
financial crisis 5–7
Financial Services Authority (FSA) 13, 86, 145, 146
Financialpost.com 59
Fix, Paul 60
Forbes.com 58, 59
Forrester 174

Franklin, Benjamin 60
French Connection 34

Gaius Petronius Arbiter 64
Galbraith, J K 59
gap analysis *see* Dice Matrix Model (DMM)
Gartner Dataquest 174
Glamour 61
Global Drug Survey 42
Goodwin, Fred 147
Google 156–59, 179
  Google Maps 177
Great Moderation 5,
Greenleaf Whittier, John 59
Guardian, The 42, 44, 48
Gunnell, Sally 51

Hansard Society 35
Harman, Charles Eustace 64
Harrods 15
Hazlitt, William 59
Health and Safety Executive 107, 183
Heath, Allister 52
Home Information Packs (HIPs) 12
Hunt, Jeremy 54
Hunt-Davis, Ben 51

ICM 22
Independent, The 28, 49, 50
  The Independent on Sunday, The 21, 31, 58
InterContinental Hotels Group 179
International Christian Resources Exhibition 182
International Telecommunication Union 178
ITV News at Ten 54

Jackson, Colin 51
James, William 61
Jefferies, Christopher 158
Jefferson, Thomas 63
John Lewis 15, 79
Johnson, Boris 18
Jung, Carl 60

Kennedy, John F 63
Keynes, J M 113
Kierkegaard, Søren 62

killer questions
  50 per cent tax bracket   90–94
  alliance of UK with US or Europe
     127–30
  Apple   141–44
  benefit system   107–12, 135–37
  'blame culture'   148–50
  debt crisis   144–48
  ethics
     deterioration of   121–24
     of large corporates   79–84
  Eurozone, future of   130–32
  gang culture   166–70
  Google and influence   156–60
  growth
     company growth   98–100
     country growth   113–17
  health and safety   103–07
  inheritance tax   132–35
  legislation and paperwork burden
     94–98
  litigation against businesses
     87–90
  manufacturing industry   117–21
  maternity leave   70–74
  next generation, help for   163–66
  offence, causing   154–56
  pay in publicly owned companies
     84–87
  pension contributions   70–74
  political correctness   100–03
  pride, in own generation   138–41
  rich/poor divide   160–62
  tax havens   67–70
  taxation   132–35
  technology and communication
     150–54
  tobacco companies   124–27
  utilities companies   75–79
King, Mervyn   5, 113
King's Cross tube fire   106
Kinnock, Neil   47

Landers, Ann   64
Lavater, Johann   60
le Carré, John   58
Lincoln, Abraham   60
London Evening Standard   60
loyalty cards   198
Lynd, R W   62

Macmillan, Harold   10
Major, John   18
marketing, in current climate
     171–74
Marks & Spencer   19
Martin, Arthur   180
MEC Entertainment   179
Mintel   21
mobile marketing
  A2P (application-to-person SMS)
     176
  statistics on   174, 176
  uses of mobiles
     apps   177
     banking and financial services
        178
     browsing and searches
        176–77
     payments   177
     subscriptions   178–78
Moynihan, David Patrick   61
MRSA   106
Murdoch, Rupert   54
Museum of London   183

National Institute for Health and
     Clinical Excellence (NICE)
     182
National Lottery   12
News Corporation   54
NewYorker.com   60
NICE (Non-Inflationary, Consistently
     Expansionary) decade   5

Observer, The   53, 62
Ogilvy, David M   61, 62
Oliver, Jamie   165
One Show, The   155
Onion, The   63
Operation Trident   168
Osborne, George   113

Page, Larry   179
Parris, Matthew   63
Pavlova, Anna   61
PayPal   181
Peoria Journal   60
'perfunctional'   49
PEST (Political, Economic, Strategic,
     Tactical) analysis   199

Peter, Laurence J 58, 62
Pierce Adams, Franklin 60
Piper Alpha 106
PricewaterhouseCoopers 52
Private Finance Initiatives (PFIs) 13

Queen Victoria 52

RealSimple.com 63
Red Tape Challenge 181
Richards, Keith 61
Rifkind, Hugo 61
Rogers, Will 61
Rolls, Charles Stewart 118
Royal Bank of Scotland (RBS) 87, 123
Royal Mail 11
Royce, Frederick Henry 118
Russell, Bertrand 59

San Francisco Chronicle 58, 62
setting up a business, challenges of 7–10
    big business 9–10
Shakespeare, William 181
Sky TV 198
Smith, Adam 113
Socrates 59
Southern Gas Network (SGN) 83
Starbucks 47
statistics
    change and assumption 27–28
    comfort zones 26–27
    community 46–48
    complaints and litigation 49–50
    contracts 54–56
    electronic waste 38–41
    employees
        as advocates 44–45
        satisfaction of 17–18
        unengaged 28–29
    engagement 35–37
    fairness 53–54
    friendliness in sales 18–21
    innovation and stigma 31–33
    logos and symbols 33–35
    marketing, power of 48–49
    parenting and working 29–31
    patriotism 52–53
    perspective 50

risk aversion 42–44
sales boundaries 21–22
servicemen, national pride in 29
sport
    athletes as inspiration 51–52
    international language of 24–26
    stakeholder engagement 45–46
    talent and categorization 23–24
    taxation 22–23
    trust and loyalty 37–38
    unemployment 41–42
Steinem, Gloria 61
Stephenson, George 118
Stoppard, Tom 60
Sun, The 47, 59
Survation 18
SWOT (Strengths, Weaknesses, Opportunities, Threats) analysis 199

Taobao 177
Thatcher, Margaret 17–18, 36, 162
Times, The 24, 38, 59, 61, 63
    Sunday Times, The 41, 47
    Times Educational Supplement 23
Twitter 172
Tyco International Ltd 69
Tynan, Kenneth 59

Unfair Contract Terms Act 1977 55
United Nations 40

Virgin 15
Voinovich, Vladimir 64
Voltaire 64

Waitrose 15
Wall Street Journal 61, 63
Wallis, Barnes 118
Warburtons 26
Waste Electrical and Electronic Equipment (WEEE) 39
Watt, James 118
Weather Channel 177
Week, The 17, 180
West Australian 62
Wharton, Edith 63

Whittle, Frank 118
Wholey, Dennis 59
Wilde, Oscar 59, 61, 63
Winchell, Walter 63
Wittgenstein, Ludwig 62

Yeates, Jo 158
YouGov 24, 47
YouTube 173, 179

Zhao, Michael 40